PETER
ROCK STAR
FROM GALILEE

PETER
ROCK STAR
FROM GALILEE

A GUIDED BIBLE STUDY FOR TEENS
AND ADULTS

SHERREE G. FUNK

© 2011 by Sherree G. Funk. Revised edition, 2014 All rights reserved.

Published by Serving One Lord Resources, 901 Blackburn Rd. Sewickley, PA

No part of this publication may be reproduced, stored in a retrieval system or transmitted in any way by any means—electronic, mechanical, photocopy, recording, or otherwise—without the prior permission of the copyright holder, except as provided by USA copyright law.

Unless otherwise noted, all Scriptures are taken from the *Holy Bible, New International Version®, NIV®.* Copyright © 1973, 1978, 1984 by Biblica, Inc.™ Used by permission of Zondervan. All rights reserved worldwide. www.zondervan.com

ISBN 13: 978-0-9823137-5-6
ISBN 10: 0-9823137-5-6
Library of Congress Catalog Card Number: 2010940633

DEDICATION

To my mother, Joyce Lorraine Anderson Goetsch,
a rock-solid Jesus-follower throughout her life.

ACKNOWLEDGMENTS

Peter has always been one of my favorite Bible characters. The Gospels, Acts, and Peter's letters provide enough about his life that we can really get to know the man and his personality. And because in many ways he is like me, impulsive and prone to pride, Peter's journey becomes my journey.

This study of Peter took longer to write than my previous studies. Maybe that was because my mom died shortly after I began. Maybe it was because I procrastinated a lot. Maybe it was that God had some things to teach me before it could be finalized. Toward the end, I wondered if I could finish at all. Only with the help of a number of wonderful people was it possible.

First, I would like to thank friends Kate Sutherland, Ann Gilbert, Kay Batt, and Theresa Butler for their strong, steadfast encouragement. Without their ever-kind words, I might have abandoned the project. I received similar encouragement and wise counsel from those who read portions of the work at the 2010 Write to Publish writer's conference. And to those who have faithfully prayed for me all along, your prayers are my strength.

I'm grateful to Amanda Griffith and her Facebook friends who critiqued the title in ways that convinced me it would work as a Bible study for teens.

I would like to thank Jayson Samuels for helpful advice on some key portions and for his foreword.

Vidar Svara kindly allowed me to photograph Mons Breidvik's beautiful 1921 painting of *Lord, Save Me!* which hangs above the altar in the Norwegian church in New Orleans.

As always, I extend a huge thank you to Todd Bolen for allowing me to use his Holy Land photos. For more great photographs, visit www.bibleplaces.com, and www.LifeintheHolyland.com Other friends and family have contributed photographs as well. Thank you all!

A big thank-you to all the students I have worked with. You continue to inspire me. My own children, Allyson, Anderson, and Anne have made helpful suggestions. And, besides the guiding Spirit of God, I have no greater support than that of my wonderful husband, Jim, both financially and emotionally, through thick and thin.

Serving One Lord,
Sherree G. Funk

CONTENTS

Foreword xi

Preface xiii

Introduction xv

Week One: Simon Joins the Band 1
    Peter drops everything to follow Jesus.

Week Two: Star Struck 15
    Jesus amazes and confuses everyone.

Week Three: Peter. Rock. 31
    Peter steps out on the stormy sea in faith.

Week Four: Rock Star Wannabe on a Rocky Road Trip 45
    Tough sledding with big promises.

Week Five: Rockslide 59
    The unthinkable happens just as Jesus said.

Week Six: Rock Steady 75
    Reconciled to Jesus, Peter inspires three thousand new believers at Pentecost.

Week Seven: Rock Star Power 87
    After miracles and prison escapes, Peter welcomes a new convert.

Week Eight: Peter. Rock. Living Stone. Star. 99
    Peter's legacy: living stones, living hope, living Word.

Photography Credits 115

FOREWORD

I was on a middle school weekend retreat at Laurelville when the message of Jesus first made sense to me. I am a pastor now and have been working with students for twenty years. I recently spoke to 450 middle school students at the same camp in the beautiful Laurel Mountains of western Pennsylvania. I was excited to teach there, remembering how that retreat so long ago changed the course and direction of my own life. Besides setting me on a path of following Jesus, it also changed my name—literally.

Before we even loaded up the church van that Friday in 1985, I ran circles around the parking lot like any prepubescent kid would do when excited. (I was thinking about the cans of shaving cream I had stashed in my duffel.) I was a gangly, happy-go-lucky kid and not too socially conscious. In other words, I was your archetypal skinny nerd minus the glasses. That year's college intern, feeling the parental stares as he futilely tried to calm the group, corralled us for a lecture on the dangers of running in the parking lot. I was fairly new to the group, so looking at me he yelled, "Hey you … (stumbling for my name) … Marty … get over here." I must have reminded him of Marty McFly, the Michael J. Fox character in the new movie, *Back to the Future*. McFly was the classic nerd.

As soon as the name rolled off his tongue, the other kids started laughing, and from that time on I was known as Marty. At first I was embarrassed, but by Sunday I had embraced my new name because it had given me a new sense of identity within the group. All weekend I was introduced to kids from other youth groups as Marty and they would laugh, but I liked it because it brought me attention that I never had before. Close friends and family still call me Marty—and I answer them.

Peter: Rock Star from Galilee is about another man whose name was changed. Peter's impulsiveness and failures make him an easy character for young men and women to relate to. As your students dive into this Bible study, I have no doubt that they will be challenged and transformed by the lessons Sherree has assembled here. I've read Sherree's other character studies and I would say that this is the best one yet! These lessons will strengthen the faith of your students and your own faith at the same time. I would suggest it for anyone who wants to grow with a group of students.

Unlike my name change, which just gave me a new nickname, biblical name changes had great significance. As Simon began to follow Jesus, he was transformed from a fisherman into a man called Peter, the rock upon which Jesus would build his church. Knowing Sherree for almost ten years now, I would say that her name has changed in my book as well. At first she was just a parent of some of my students, then she became a trusted friend, and now I would call her a peer in ministry to students.

—Jayson Samuels
Co-Founder and Family Pastor, NorthBridge Community Church
Cranberry, Pennsylvania

PREFACE

I have always loved hymns and praise music. As a little girl, I memorized multiple verses of dozens of hymns. As an adult, when contemporary Christian music came of age, I kept Christian radio playing in my car. When my children were young, Houston's KSBJ played the music we sang along to during carpool. Music has a way of speaking to the heart, and the message lingers long after spoken or written words have been forgotten.

As I began writing *Peter: Rock Star from Galilee,* I kept noticing how some of my favorite Christian songs fit beautifully with lessons about Peter. Some songs refer to specific incidents in Peter's life, some speak to feelings Peter might have had, and some link lessons Peter learned to life in today's world.

With iTunes and iPods, today's teenagers are wired for music most of the time. So each chapter of this Bible study starts with a playlist of songs. Incorporating music with study is a great way to make spiritual lessons stick.

Play it. Sing it. Live it.

HOW IS THIS STUDY GUIDE SET UP?

Each of the eight chapters has the following:

 A playlist in which each song pertains in some way to the lessons of the week. Try listening to them, paying attention to the lyrics.

A preview of the week's study and a prayer to set you off in the right direction.

Five days of study with interactive, short-answer questions.

 'Chew on this' questions for deeper thought.

 Christian Reality Challenges for hands-on faith building.

XIII

INTO MY LIFE—your guide for the small-group meeting, including:

 The Jam Session, a condensed list of questions for small-group discussion.

 A replay summary of the week and a final prayer.

MESSAGE TO STUDENTS

You will get the most from your study if you put in thirty minutes a day for five days each week. Of course, that is an average; you could do it all in a concentrated effort of two and a half hours. You might want to work out some questions on the phone with a friend. You may end up doing some questions together as a group. Some of you may be using this as part of your homeschool curriculum. Others may be doing this with a parent or mentor. Come together with a small group and discuss your thoughts. Your friends may have found something you missed, or you may give them something to think about.

The Bible is not meant to be read only on Sundays. When you open it during a private quiet time, you invite God to speak directly to you through his Word. Then your own personal journey in discipleship really begins.

MESSAGE TO LEADERS

You will find this study easy to lead if you do the workbook yourself ahead of time. Look over Into My Life before you meet with your group so you can be ready to lead discussion. You probably won't have time to discuss every question, but choose those that can benefit the teens in your particular group.

Be prepared to help your group with the Christian Reality Challenges. Many of these are practical projects involving service to others. This might mean suggesting ideas, making phone calls, or soliciting help from your church's ministries. These projects are instrumental in getting kids to internalize what they are learning.

Try to listen to at least one of the songs on the playlist and be ready to talk about the lyrics. Locate a YouTube video of the song, either a concert version or just a posting of the lyrics, and consider showing it to your group. Encourage students to listen for other songs that relate to the week's material, either on Christian radio, in church, or from their own music collections. Some secular songs may relate as well.

Encourage students to collect eight songs for a personal CD, one from each week. This will be a reminder of all they have learned about Peter and discipleship.

If your youth group is doing the study in small groups and you have a large group gathering, consider using a song or two from the weekly playlist for your worship time.

Thank you for taking time to lead a group of students in Bible study. You are taking the admonition in Psalm 78:4 seriously: "We will tell the next generation the praiseworthy deeds of the Lord, his power and the wonders he has done." I pray that God will bless you richly.

FOR MORE INFORMATION

Additional materials, links, and color photos are available at the Serving One Lord website, www.servingonelord.com

INTRODUCTION

If the New Testament were a Broadway musical, Peter would be one of the stars. The superstar was Jesus Christ, but Peter would be a rock star. Peter attracted attention by doing outrageous things; he was a "sinful man" by his own admission. Emotional, impetuous, and edgy, Peter spiced up the stories of Jesus. He thought he could be the best disciple, but even his best intentions led to miserable failure. Then following the resurrection, after a special beach breakfast with Jesus, Peter's career took off. He performed miracles, drew crowds, preached to thousands, got busted by the Pharisees, and broke down the Jew-Gentile barrier. And he did it all for the sake of Jesus. From a rickety fishing boat on Lake Galilee, to the grand courts of Herod's Temple, to the villages of Joppa and Caesarea, Peter rocked the world around him.

We love Peter as much for his fears and failures as for the times he got it right. If impulsive Peter could become a rock-solid disciple, maybe there is hope for us too. Join me as we explore Peter's bumpy road to stardom in light of his tight friendship with the God-man, Jesus.

Each week of the Bible study begins with a list of songs whose lyrics pertain to the week's study. Listen to them if you can. Five days of guided study follow. It works best if you answer the questions on your own before gathering weekly with your small group. And each week ends with a set of discussion questions for your group. Pray that God will speak to you personally as you study.

Before you begin, take time to get to know the others in your study group. Write everyone's name on the blank page opposite and jot down whatever short prayer each person requests.

WEEK ONE

SIMON JOINS THE BAND

So they pulled their boats up on shore, left everything and followed him.
—Luke 5:11

PLAYLIST

Do you like music? Who doesn't? Find some of these songs and listen to the lyrics. Some you can find in a hymn book, some you can buy and download from iTunes, some you may have on CD, and many have YouTube videos. Use them to warm you up for Bible study, in student worship, or enjoy them in your small group. Each week find at least one song that helps you remember something from the week's study. Then put all eight together on a personal CD recounting Peter's faith journey.

> I Will Follow – Chris Tomlin
> I Have Decided to Follow Jesus – Third Day
> Fishers of Men – Rhonda Vincent
> Sea of Souls – Michael Card
> We Will Follow – Jars of Clay
> I Will Make You Fishers of Men – traditional hymn
> I Will Follow – By The Tree

WEEK ONE PREVIEW

When Simon Peter decides to try something completely new, everyone pays attention. This week we look at his dramatic decision to leave the fishing business and accompany Jesus full time. Like many of us, Peter knew who Jesus was for a while before this fateful day. Let's see what made the difference in choosing to follow.

Dear Father, If you are calling me, please make it clear. What will I have to leave?
Will it be worth it? What will my friends and family say? Do you really want me to follow you? Amen.

PETER: ROCK STAR FROM GALILEE

WEEK ONE, DAY ONE
GONE FISHIN'

Long before he met Jesus, Peter was a full-time fisherman. Let's try to get into the head of a guy who loves to fish. Why do people like to fish today? Some want an excuse to get away from parents or family. Competitive types want bragging rights for landing "the big one." For some, the quiet time in a natural setting is attractive, and for some, fishing brings back memories of good times with a father, brother, or friend. Some enjoy the fancy equipment, like the fly-fisherman with all his real-looking flies. Personally, I just love the smell and taste of fresh trout cooked on an open fire.

Ever go fishing? What did you like about it?

_____

Not simply a sport fisherman, Peter fished for a living. He knew the ropes; he had probably been fishing every day for most of his life. Commercial fishing, even today, is one of the most dangerous professions. Fishermen like Peter were more than just strong. They had to know more than one language perhaps, have good business sense, and be able to react quickly to changing weather conditions. They had to cooperate with others in the community in order to maintain a good market for their fish. The first men to follow Jesus were fishermen.

Do you know anyone in the commercial fishing business? What are they like?

_____

Why do you think Jesus chose fishermen as his first disciples?

_____

Put a star beside any of these characteristics you think would also make a good disciple.
- ❏ strong
- ❏ brave
- ❏ practical
- ❏ morning person
- ❏ patient
- ❏ hard-working
- ❏ not easily discouraged
- ❏ community-oriented
- ❏ cooperative
- ❏ multilingual

WEEK ONE, DAY TWO
PLENTY OF FISH IN THE SEA

Galilean fishermen used long, wooden, oar-driven boats, with or without a sail. They fished mainly with nets, dragging them behind the boats or between two boats. Skilled fishermen could bring in massive amounts of fish if they came across a school without spooking them. To go undetected by the fish, Peter and his partners, James and John, often fished at night. At dawn they pulled in to shore, exhausted, to clean and put away their nets.

THE SEA OF GALILEE BOAT

Reconstructed 1st Century Boat

In 1986, when drought produced record low water in the Sea of Galilee, some fishermen spotted the outline of a wooden boat buried in the mud near the city of Magdala. Carbon dating of artifacts near the boat pointed to a first century age. Archaeologist Shelley Wachsmann and his team excavated the boat and soaked it for seven years in a bath of polyethylene glycol. Finally, the wood was sufficiently preserved to survive exposure to air. The boat is now on display in the YigalAllon Centre.

Could this boat have been used by Peter? No one can know for sure. Yet the age is right, it was found very near Capernaum, and it is the type of boat Peter would have fished from. At twenty-six by seven feet, it could have held up to fifteen men. The reconstructed boat helps us visualize the many Gospel stories involving fishing boats on Galilee.

www.jesusboatmuseum.com

The Sea of Galilee Boat: A 2000 Year Old Discovery from the Sea of Legends, (1995, 2000), Shelley Wachsmann, Professor of Anthropology at Texas A&M University.

PETER: ROCK STAR FROM GALILEE

Read Luke 5:1–11 for a glimpse into the life of Peter the fisherman. First, who is this man Simon in the text? You thought this was a study of Peter! Jesus changed Simon's name to Peter a bit later. For now, any reference to Simon is a reference to Peter the fisherman.

> Jesus asked Simon to row the boat away from the shore a little bit while he was teaching. Why do you think Jesus suggested this?
> ❑ He wanted to get away from the people for a while.
> ❑ He wanted to go for a swim.
> ❑ Everyone could see and hear better if he was fifteen to twenty feet from shore.
> ❑ Jesus wanted to keep Peter from hurrying home to bed.

After Jesus finished teaching, he told Peter to row again out into the deep water. Give at least two reasons Peter probably wouldn't want to do this.

_____

_____

_____

> What happened in verses 6–7 when the fishermen did as Jesus asked?
> ❑ Nothing.
> ❑ They caught a few fish and headed home for breakfast.
> ❑ Two boats started sinking from all the fish they caught.
> ❑ The nets began to tear.
> ❑ The fishermen had to call for help.

Now this was more than amazing. Despite their exhaustion and frustration, Peter and the others did exactly what Jesus asked. And then, what a catch!

CHEW ON THIS: *Sometimes the greatest blessing comes when we do the one thing God asks us to do, even if we don't really want to. When have you found that statement to be true?*

WEEK ONE, DAY THREE
WHAT A CATCH!

How did Jesus know all those fish were there? It was a miracle! This catch would bring in a lot of money at the market. But seeing all the fish, Peter reacted in a strange way.

What did Peter do and what did he say in Luke 5:8? _____

_____

I wonder why Peter said this to Jesus. Imagine how you would feel if something like this happened to you.

What are some things you might have said? _____

_____

So, why this, "Go away. I'm a sinful man"? What do you think? _____

_____

I might have said, "Hey, why don't you join us every time we go fishing? You could be our foolproof fish finder! You're a lucky charm!"

Peter sensed that this Jesus was more than just a lucky charm. He couldn't believe this amazing man wanted to be his friend. Peter suddenly felt the need to confess. I wonder if just being around Jesus made him more aware of his bad habits.

CHEW ON THIS: *What makes people want to push Jesus away today?*

Then Jesus responded in a strange way. What does Jesus say to Peter in Luke 5:10?

___

Matthew records a slightly different version of this story. What's different about Jesus' response in Matthew 4:18–20?

___

At this point Peter has nothing to say. He's probably busy trying to unravel what Jesus means. What do you think Jesus meant?

___

But Peter's life has surely changed. How do we know this? Luke 5:11 and Matthew 4:20 give the answer.

CHEW ON THIS: *What made Peter change his mind and go with Jesus? What can we do to make people change their minds about Jesus?*

CAPERNAUM

Aerial view of modern octagonal church with ancient synagogue on right.

Franciscan church.

Ruins of Peter's house beneath church.

Capernaum, on the north shore of the Sea of Galilee, was strategically located on the Via Maris, a major trade route running from Damascus, Syria, along the Mediterranean coast to Egypt.

The population of 1000 to 1500 was enough to support a synagogue, a wide main street, and many large homes with courtyards. One of those homes is thought to have been the home of Peter. A fourth century church was built atop a house church from the first century, widely believed to have been Peter's house.

At the beautiful Franciscan church built over the site, pilgrims may look down through a glass floor into the ruins of Peter's house. And the church's windows afford a lovely view of the Sea of Galilee, where so many Gospel stories took place.
(Photos by Todd Bolen, www.BiblePlaces.com)

WEEK ONE, DAY FOUR
DO I KNOW YOU?

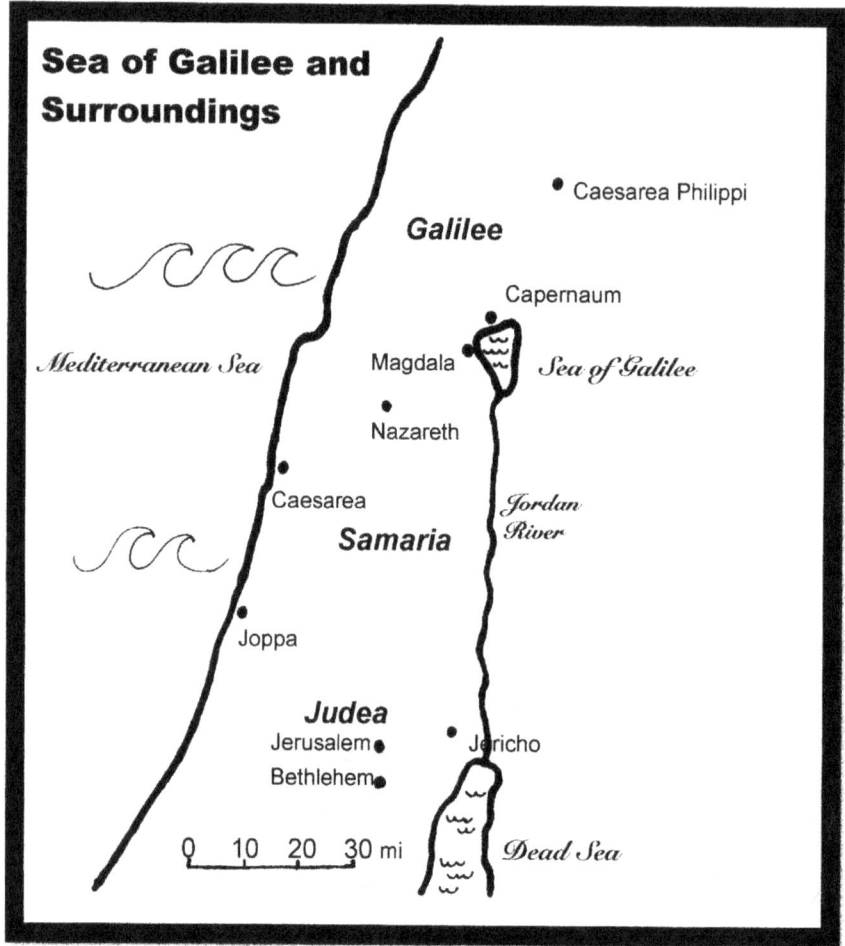

The morning of the outrageous fish-catch was not the first time Peter had met Jesus. After all, they were neighbors.

> According to Matthew 4:13, where did Jesus and Peter live? _____
> Can you circle it on the map?

Perhaps when Jesus moved to Capernaum, Peter showed him around. Peter's house has been excavated in Capernaum, and a beautiful church has been built on the site.

In Luke 4:38–39, Jesus visited Peter at home in Capernaum after synagogue one day. What did he do that day at Peter's house?
- ❏ Watched football on TV
- ❏ Chatted about the fishing business
- ❏ Healed Peter's sick mother-in-law
- ❏ Ate hot dogs for lunch

SIMON JOINS THE BAND

John 1:35–42 tells how Peter met Jesus down by the Jordan River, where John the Baptist was preaching and baptizing. According to this passage, who introduced Peter to Jesus? _____

So it seems that Jesus and Peter were already acquainted. Jesus even told Simon that he would be called Peter before he really knew him very well. Based on these passages (Luke 4 and John 1), what things did Peter know about Jesus before the miraculous fish-catch?

_____

_____

Peter knew who Jesus was. He had seen and heard about many miracles already. He saw the crowds pressing close to hear what Jesus said. His brother Andrew had seen John pointing toward Jesus when he said, "Look, the Lamb of God." Andrew had insisted that Peter meet Jesus, and he did. But all that was just background knowledge until the day Jesus climbed into his boat. That was when their relationship changed.

What have *you* heard about Jesus? What do you know about him? _____

_____

Has Jesus done anything *just for you* that compares to what he did for Peter? _____

_____

Is Jesus in your boat? _____

Sometimes we need a personal experience to really believe. It's one thing to hear that many people follow Jesus. You may have close friends or family members who believe, but until Jesus comes into your boat and demonstrates his love for you personally, you may not really get it. When Jesus went with Peter that day, He didn't just rock Peter's fishing boat; he rocked his world.

CHRISTIAN REALITY CHALLENGE: *Be an Andrew. Be the one to invite someone to Bible study or worship, then watch to see what God will do to get into that person's boat. Ask Jesus to get in your boat. Tell him you are sinful, but that you are willing to trust him, to follow him. See what he does.*

WEEK ONE, DAY FIVE
YOU LEAD; I'LL FOLLOW

It was a big decision to drop everything and go with Jesus, but Peter was not alone.

According to Matthew 4:18–22, who else besides Peter decided to follow Jesus? _____

_____

Read Luke 5:27–28. Who else? _____ (This guy named Levi is the same as Matthew who wrote the gospel.)

Now there were five people following Jesus. What businesses did they leave? _____

_____

You may already know there were more than five disciples. Some are famous for bit parts in the Gospels and Acts. Some we don't know much about. For a complete list, read Luke 6:12–16 and write all the names below. Put a star by the ones you have heard of.

_____   _____

_____   _____

_____   _____

_____   _____

_____   _____

_____   _____

SIMON JOINS THE BAND

Besides being called disciples, these twelve were also called what? (Luke 6:13)
- ❏ Jesus freaks
- ❏ apostles
- ❏ the Band
- ❏ crazy

From this point on, throughout the three years of Jesus' ministry until his arrest and crucifixion, Peter followed Jesus. His named topped every list of disciples. Everywhere Jesus went, Peter tried to keep up. He saw all the miracles, heard what Jesus taught, and asked tough questions. Peter didn't always fully understand what was happening or what Jesus was driving at, but he stayed close. He wanted to learn all he could from Jesus.

What did Peter say in Luke 18:28? _____

If you had been Peter, would you have left everything to follow Jesus?
- ❏ Yes, because Jesus was just amazing.
- ❏ Only if my friends went too.
- ❏ Maybe, after thinking about it.
- ❏ No, I really don't think I could have done that.

Do you think Jesus expects us to leave everything to follow him today? _____

Read Luke 9:57–62. What does this passage say about the cost of following Jesus?

_____

In your opinion, what are some of the risks and benefits associated with following Jesus today?

Risks: _____

_____

Benefits: _____

_____

CHEW ON THIS: *What kind of person does Jesus call? Are you the type of person he might be calling? What does it take to be a follower of Jesus?*

It seems that Jesus calls people to simply follow him. He wants people who won't make excuses or put other things first, people who won't ignore him, people who are willing to take some exciting chances and change their perspective. Peter was gung ho. Enthusiastic. Ready to rock and roll. Are you?

CHEW ON THIS: *If you were doing something you love doing (like sports, video games, or watching TV) and Jesus came to you and said, "Follow me," would you stop doing the thing you love to do?*

CHRISTIAN REALITY CHALLENGE: *Follow Jesus for a whole day. Think about him every step of your day. Do what you think he would do. Act like you think he would act. Give up what he would want you to give up, just for one day. This is actually harder than you think. Share your experiences with your group the next time you meet.*

Could you do this every day?
- ❑ no way
- ❑ not successfully
- ❑ only if Jesus helps me
- ❑ sure, no problem

SIMON JOINS THE BAND

WEEK ONE: INTO MY LIFE

Jesus is calling me to follow him, but ...

JAM SESSION

Discussion questions for your small group. Jam on!

1. What makes people want to push Jesus away today?

2. What makes people change their minds, turn around, and follow Jesus?

3. What can we do to encourage people to change their minds about Jesus?

4. What kind of person does Jesus call? What does it take to be a follower of Jesus?

5. Will following Jesus require you to change what you are doing? How?

6. Which songs from the playlist are most meaningful to you as you reflect on Peter's call to follow?

CHRISTIAN REALITY CHALLENGES

Be an Andrew.

Ask Jesus into your life.

Follow Jesus fully for a day.

 WEEK ONE REPLAY

Peter may not have been sure what he was getting himself into. He was a bit reluctant to get close to such a godly, powerful person as Jesus. He tried to push Jesus away, but the love he felt from Jesus, the genuine friendship, the miracles of fish—all of this made him want to follow, and he willingly gave up his fishing business for the opportunity. In the same way, will you give it a try? Jesus wants to have a BFF relationship with you too.

*Dear Jesus, I want to follow you. Please show me the first step …
and then the next … and the next.
I know I will make mistakes, for I am sinful,
but I am willing to give up some of my habits
and desires just to be with you. Take me with you on a discipleship trip.
I want to join your band. Amen.*

WEEK TWO

STAR STRUCK

*Everyone was amazed and gave praise to God.
They were filled with awe and said, "We have seen remarkable things today."*

—Luke 5:26

PLAYLIST

Living Water – Bob Carlisle
Praise You in This Storm – Casting Crowns
Tell Me the Stories of Jesus – traditional hymn
Heaven in His Eyes – Rich Mullins
Miracles – Newsboys

WEEK TWO PREVIEW

After leaving his fishing business, Peter started spending a lot of time with Jesus. Jesus was just so, well, different. He was always doing things that surprised, confused, or amazed the disciples. When they weren't scratching their heads, they were shocked and awed by Jesus' power and teaching. But as Jesus' popularity grew, the disciples were glad to be associated with him—at least until the going got rough.

Such reactions to Jesus are still pretty common. Whenever you start spending a lot of time with Jesus, you find yourself in uncertain territory. Suddenly, many things you thought were absolutes are up for reinterpretation. This week, imagine you are one of the original disciples, watching Jesus begin his ministry. We will take a look at several surprising aspects of Jesus' early ministry that had a big influence on Peter's new faith. Think about how they would have affected you.

Dear Jesus, You are so amazing. I don't understand all that you say or why you do some of the things you do, but show me your power. Show me your love. Help me understand who you really are. Amen.

PETER: ROCK STAR FROM GALILEE

WEEK TWO, DAY ONE
WHERE'S JESUS?

It wasn't long before crowds came, looking for Jesus to heal their many illnesses and diseases. Jesus even cast out evil spirits, giving many insane people a return to their right mind.

Read Mark 1:29–34. This is a story we read last week in Luke. In Mark's account of the healing of Peter's mother-in-law, how did Jesus heal her? _____

What did he do in verse 31? _____

Word got out very fast, and that same evening after sunset, a lot happened at Peter's house. Who stopped by Peter's house that night?
- ❑ a couple of sick friends
- ❑ his fishing buddies
- ❑ the whole town of Capernaum
- ❑ all the sick and demon-possessed

I imagine it turned into a pretty late night for Jesus and for Peter. The house was overrun with sick people wanting to be healed. And Jesus healed them, giving each one the love and attention they needed. Luke 4:40 says Jesus laid his hands on each one.

After a late night with friends, what would you be doing the next morning?

_____

Now read Mark 1:35–38. What was Jesus doing? _____

I imagine Peter and the disciples woke up to loud knocks at the door when more people arrived, looking for the miraculous healer. Peter noticed Jesus was not in the house and went running to look for him. After all, Peter was accustomed to early mornings and hard work so he probably thought, "Good. More medical work for Jesus… Let's get busy. Nothing's more important than healing these people. Now, where is Jesus?"

But when he found his friend praying quietly, what do you think ran through his mind?

_____

_____

How would you have reacted? _____

Jesus was praying? Was prayer more important than working miracles of healing? Did Jesus need to pray? Though Peter may not have realized it right away, Jesus was showing him that prayer is important, *especially* when we are doing God's work. When we are under a lot of pressure, when we have worked late into the night and have more to do the next day, we need, more than ever, to take time for prayer. Prayer is God's way of keeping us focused, encouraged, and calm.

CHEW ON THIS: *When you are feeling the pressure, do you still make time to pray?* _____

Why or why not? _____

If we are like Peter, eager to *do* what needs to be done, we sometimes jump in without thinking, and often without praying. Jesus surprised his followers when he took time to pray.

CHRISTIAN REALITY CHALLENGE: *This week, pray every morning before you start your day.*

WEEK TWO, DAY TWO
LIVING WATER

Jesus Speaks with The Samaritan Woman, by Danish artist, Carl Heinrich Bloch (1834-1890)

Another time, Jesus and the disciples traveled through Samaria on their way back to Capernaum from Judea. Normally, Jews did not travel through this area because they pretty much hated the Samaritans who lived there. It was a prejudice, just like racial or religious bias in our day. In order to avoid "those people," most Jews crossed the Jordan River, walked up the east bank, and re-crossed the Jordan only when they had completely passed by Samaria. So it was a bit of a surprise when Jesus insisted they go through Samaria. Jesus stopped and sat down beside a well at about lunchtime, while the disciples went into town for lunch.

While Jesus sat beside the well, a Samaritan woman carrying a large jar came alone to draw water. Jesus asked her for a drink. The wonderful conversation Jesus had with this woman is recorded in John 4:1–26. Read it now.

According to John 4:27, what surprised Peter and the disciples when they returned?

_____

_____

Jesus then made a surprising statement in John 4:32. What did he say to them?

_____

_____

What do you think he was talking about? _____

_____

What surprises you most about this encounter? _____

I was surprised Jesus knew all about her past. I was surprised when he told her straight out that he was the Messiah. He usually tried to keep that quiet. And I was surprised at how she responded to his kindness.

CHEW ON THIS: *What surprises you about Jesus? Be honest.* _____

_____

CHRISTIAN REALITY CHALLENGE: *Surprise someone with kind conversation: a little kid, an elderly person, your school principal, someone you usually ignore. Share challenge results with your group next week.*

THE DIRTY PARABLE

Jesus didn't teach like most teachers. For one thing, he was never boring. He didn't just repeat the dos and don'ts of the law, like most of the religious leaders. He taught mainly in parables. A parable is a story with a hidden point or purpose. The word *parable* comes from the Greek work *paraboe*, which means "a placing beside," like a comparison or illustration. I like to think of a parabola, a geometric curve which is defined by a point but does not pass directly through that point. Like a parabola, a parable skirts around the point of the story, but doesn't spell it out. Parables make you think a little.

Jesus told a parable that confused the disciples. It's called the parable of the sower. Read it first in Matthew 13:1–9. Then read the same story in Luke 8:4–8.

What four types of soil does the seed fall on?

1. _____ 2. _____
3. _____ 4. _____

And what does the seed represent? _____

OK. The disciples have some questions, understandably. One big question is found in Matthew 13:10–17.

It seems Jesus taught in parables *because* it would be a little confusing. What? Let's get this straight. He wanted the lesson to be hidden? How would you have reacted to this if you were Peter? I would have been scratching my head.

CHEW ON THIS: *Why might Jesus want his lessons hidden in parables?*

Then Jesus explained the parable. See Luke 8:11–15. Was he really talking about planting seeds in a garden? Or was he talking about something else altogether?

Can you summarize the parable in your own words? _____

What does the seed represent? _____

What kind of soil are you? _____

What kind do you want to be? _____

I bet Peter wanted to be good soil too. He wanted to have a noble and good heart; to hear and retain the words of Jesus; and by persevering, to produce a crop, even a hundred-fold. At first, though, Peter found Jesus' lessons confusing. There was so much to learn from this teacher.

CHEW ON THIS: *Do you think some things in the Bible only make sense when people are open to the things of God? Does faith or an attitude of openness help you understand more?*

_____

_____

WEEK TWO, DAY THREE
AMAZING!

Which is more amazing: a delicious cupcake or a juicy cheeseburger, your team in the Super Bowl or landing a ticket to the game, a record-breaking swim time or a full-court basket at the buzzer, *The Amazing Race* or "Amazing Grace?" All these things (except grace, which is truly amazing) are pretty tame compared to some things Jesus did. Let's take a look at three incidents which astound us even today.

One time, after a day of teaching and healing, Jesus suggested they all hop in the boat and sail across the lake. And just like *The Minnow* on the TV show, *Gilligan's Island*, "the tiny ship was tossed."

Have you ever been in a boat during a storm? What happened? _____
Share your experience with your group.

Which of the following might happen to a small boat in a storm?
- ❑ boat capsizes
- ❑ passengers get wet
- ❑ passengers get flipped out of boat
- ❑ lightning strikes boat
- ❑ boat gets blown off course
- ❑ shipwreck
- ❑ sails tear or masts break from the force of the wind
- ❑ boat takes on water (waves break over the edge of the boat)
- ❑ hypothermia (passengers freeze in the cold water)
- ❑ passengers drown

Now read Mark 4:35–41 for what happened on this little cruise across the lake. No, they were not shipwrecked on an island, but …

What did Mark call this storm?
❏ a light drizzle   ❏ a furious squall   ❏ a hurricane   ❏ a blizzard

Which of the things described above were happening to the crew of disciples?
_____
_____

Where was Jesus, and what was he doing? _____

A calm Sea of Galilee with storm clouds brewing

Because the Sea of Galilee is shallow (less than two hundred feet deep) and sits in a steep-sided valley, the usually calm water whips up into violent waves when the weather changes. Winds funnel into the lake area through narrow canyons on either side, and cool air masses collide with the warmer air in the basin, which is seven hundred feet below sea level. So when you set sail on the Sea of Galilee, you don't know if the glassy surface will remain calm until you reach your destination. Apparently, one of those sudden storms caught the disciples by surprise.

As a seasoned fisherman, Peter knew the dangers of these sudden squalls. He and the others rushed to wake Jesus, who was unbelievably *asleep*. They were terrified of possibly drowning with the next big wave. Amazingly, Jesus never panicked. He just took care of the problem.

What did he do? _____
_____

Everyone was still terrified even after the wind had calmed completely. What did they ask each other in verse 41? _____

If Jesus could even command the forces of nature to be still, who could he be but God? I think it's safe to say the disciples, including Peter, were totally amazed. Wouldn't you be?

CHEW ON THIS: *Does God have power over the weather today? Can he redirect a hurricane? Stop a tornado? When does God use that power and when does he withhold it? Remember, God's ways are not our ways, and we may not ever see the full picture.*

Jesus Sleeping During the Tempest, by French artist James Tissot (1836-1902)

WEEK TWO, DAY FOUR
UP ON THE ROOFTOP

In Capernaum one day, Jesus preached to a packed house. People crowded in and blocked the door. Pharisees and religious bigwigs from as far away as Jerusalem listened intently. Jesus healed many sick and diseased persons, as he often did. Four guys who had heard of Jesus' healing power brought their paralyzed friend who could not walk.

Read Luke 5:17–20. Since the door was blocked, how did they get in? _____

That unusual entrance stopped everything as dust and little pieces of the roof fell in. Everyone's eyes widened when the pallet came down into the room. Jesus, not the least bit irritated, was concentrating on the four guys. They were risking their own safety by climbing up on the roof carrying a stretcher to lay their friend right in front of Jesus.

When he saw the obvious confidence and faith of them all he said:
- ❑ "Wow, you guys must be crazy."
- ❑ "I'm trying to teach right now. Could you come back later?"
- ❑ "Get up and walk."
- ❑ "Friend, your sins are forgiven."

Well, *that* was pretty amazing, because pretty much everybody knew that only God can forgive sins, and God's forgiveness at the time called for lots of special sacrifices. The religious leaders who witnessed this incident thought they knew more about God than anybody else. They were offended. They called it *blasphemy*.

Look up blasphemy in a dictionary. What does it mean? _____

After reading the rest of the story in Luke 5:21–26, summarize what Jesus said to the Pharisees.

_____
_____

And then, turning to the paralyzed guy on the mat, Jesus said, "Get up, take your mat, and go home." So if Jesus could heal a paralyzed man, could he also forgive sins?

What had to be true if Jesus could do both?
- ❑ He was a great magician.
- ❑ He was a good doctor, but a blasphemer.
- ❑ He was related to or in touch with God himself.

According to verse 26, what did everyone think after this incident?
- ❑ They were amazed.   ❑ They were filled with awe.
- ❑ They praised God.   ❑ They thought it was remarkable.

🦴 **CHEW ON THIS:** *Which would have amazed you more, the paralyzed man walking or the authority of Jesus? Why?*

By now, Peter and the others could see that Jesus was capable of wonders beyond imagination. But he was also creating controversy with the Jewish leaders. That was only the beginning. They hadn't seen anything yet.

RAISING THE DEAD?

While walking along the streets of Capernaum, the synagogue ruler, Jairus, stopped Jesus and asked him to come heal his daughter, who was very sick, even dying.

Read Mark 5:21–24. Did this man believe Jesus could make his little girl well? _____

Read Mark 5:35–36 to see what happened next. What did Jesus say to Jairus after the servants ran up to report the girl's death?
- ❏ "Oops, we'd better hurry."
- ❏ "I'll see what I can do."
- ❏ "Sorry, I couldn't help it."
- ❏ "Don't be afraid, just believe."

Now finish the story by reading Mark 5:37–43. When they got to Jairus's house, who went in with Jesus? _____

What happened when Jesus took the hand of the twelve-year-old girl? _____

How would you have felt if you were Peter? _____

How would you feel if you were that girl? _____

Naturally, Peter and the others were astonished. Wouldn't you be? This Jesus could command the wind, heal paralyzed people, forgive sins, and even bring the dead back to life. Amazing! It seemed like everywhere Jesus went, he did something shocking. Peter was trying to understand. He stayed as close to Jesus as possible. He listened.

🦴 **CHEW ON THIS:** *If Jesus could do these amazing miracles like healing sick people, raising some back to life from death, why would the religious leaders despise him? Can you think of any situation in the world today in which someone who does good things for people is despised by religious leaders or government leaders?*

WEEK TWO, DAY FIVE
BREAD FOR EVERYONE

Let's imagine how Peter himself might have told this next amazing story.

"I'll never forget that day. We had just returned from our first assignment. Jesus had sent us, two-by-two, into the villages. Incredibly, we were able to drive out demons in the name of Jesus and even heal people of awful diseases. I was so glad I had followed him. Now we were pretty tired and Jesus could tell. He thought we needed some rest, so we took the boat out. But huge crowds of people, seeing us set sail, ran along the lakeshore so they could meet us when we landed.

"So much for the little retreat we were hoping for. The people eagerly listened to Jesus speak. Some were sick, of course, in need of Jesus's healing. And Jesus never turned anyone away. He never seemed to mind the interruptions. He had compassion. We were all tired and hungry. No one had packed lunch, there had been no time to fish, and it was late in the afternoon.

"We suggested Jesus send the people away to find dinner, but do you know what he said? He told us to give them something to eat! He knew we didn't have any food. What was he thinking? I was puzzled, as usual. Philip said out loud what we were all thinking: 'Eight months wages wouldn't buy enough food for each one to have a bite!'

"My brother Andrew had been talking to a boy who had a small lunch and was willing to share. But we knew it wasn't enough for so many. We estimated there were about five thousand people.

"Jesus took that boy's lunch (just five small rolls and two fish), gave thanks to God for it, and we began to feed the crowd. It was the most amazing thing yet. Believe it or not, everyone got something to eat. There was even more left over when everyone had enough. Twelve baskets of bread were collected at the end—one for each of us.

"I was beginning to believe Jesus could do anything. I had seen him heal people of horrible diseases. I had watched as dead people were made alive again. He could command winds to cease, and now he made bread multiply for hungry crowds. He could be the new king of Israel and free us from the Roman government, but he didn't want that; he seemed to avoid the spotlight. He taught as if he knew just what God was thinking, but the religious leaders were always irritated when they heard him. I wanted to learn everything he could teach me. I wanted to show him that I trusted him."

According to John 6:14–15, what were the other people thinking? _____

CHEW ON THIS: *Hunger is still a big issue in our world today. What would Jesus say to you about that? How would he expect you to share your abundance with others?*

CHRISTIAN REALITY CHALLENGE: *Do something for hungry people. Use your imagination and do something as a group if you can. Make it a rock-star worthy attempt! Here are some possibilities:*

Collect food for a local food bank.
Raise money for a world humanitarian group such as World Vision.
Prepare and feed dinner to the homeless in your city.

REVIEW

Take a minute to review this week's lesson. Below is a list of all the Jesus stories we looked at this week.

Which of these seven stories impresses or amazes you the most? Put a star beside it. Which one gives you a better idea of who Jesus was? Put an I beside it. Which one makes you love Jesus more? Put a heart beside it.

- ❏ Jesus praying alone
- ❏ Jesus talking to the woman at the well
- ❏ Jesus teaching in parables
- ❏ Jesus calming the storm
- ❏ Jesus forgiving sins and healing the paralyzed man
- ❏ Jesus raising Jairus's dead daughter
- ❏ Jesus feeding five thousand people with just a small lunch

Share your answers with your study group when you meet.

WEEK TWO: INTO MY LIFE

How do the stories of Jesus impact me?

JAM SESSION

- Jesus prayed early in the morning, even when he was extremely busy. How can you follow his example?

- What surprises you about Jesus? Be honest.

- Do you think some things in the Bible don't make sense to people who are not open to the things of God? Does faith or an attitude of openness help you understand more?

- Which amazes you more: that Jesus can heal people miraculously or that he really forgives sinners?

- Why did the religious leaders have a problem with Jesus healing people?

- There is a saying: "No good deed goes unpunished." Do you agree? In 2008, an incident seemed to prove the point. A fifteen-year-old girl in California felt ill during her bus ride to school and wanted to return home. The bus driver agreed to take her home after the elementary school bus run. During that run, the bus driver unexpectedly fell off her seat and hit her head. The sick girl leaped up and bravely managed to stop the bus safely. The girl received detention for not following the proper procedure for leaving school with an illness. (She didn't check in with the office, call parents, etc.) She was punished for the rules she broke, in spite of the good she did. Can you think of any other situation in the world today in which someone who does good things for people is punished in some way? Does that make you want to avoid doing good things?

- Hunger is still a big issue in our world today. All of us in America are rich and fat compared with the rest of the world. Over a billion people in the world live on less than one dollar a day. How would Jesus expect you to share your abundance with others?

- What new thing did you learn about Jesus this week?

- Which song from the playlist best portrays Jesus?

CHRISTIAN REALITY CHALLENGES

Pray before you start your day.

Surprise someone with kindness.

Feed hungry people.

 WEEK TWO REPLAY

Jesus lived an incredible life on earth. Every step he took, every miracle, every word out of his mouth had a purpose. Peter was lucky enough to live and eat with Jesus. Fortunately for us, four gospel accounts provide plenty of material from which to learn. To be a disciple of Jesus, we look to Jesus himself, allowing his life to impact how we live ours. Can you see him?

Dear Jesus, I am amazed at the things you did. You had authority over sickness, bad weather, even death. And you had love and compassion for everyone. You showed everyone what God is really like. I want to know more about you. I want you in my life. Make me open to your ways. Amen.

WEEK THREE

PETER. ROCK.

I tell you that you are Peter and on this rock I will build my church.

—Matthew 16:18

PLAYLIST

Walk on the Water – Britt Nicole
You Never Let Go – Matt Redman
The Transfiguration – SufjanStevens
Step by Step – Rich Mullins
Transfiguration Hymn – Ken Bible
Could You Be Messiah? – Gary Valenciano
Glorious – Newsboys

WEEK THREE PREVIEW

After a couple of years of hanging with Jesus—watching his miracles and listening to his open-air lessons—Peter thought he was ready for something. He was beginning to understand Jesus. From the healing miracles to the counter-intuitive teaching to the boundless compassion, Peter could tell Jesus was a true classic, unlike any teacher he had ever heard. Jesus' full identity was not yet perfectly clear, but Peter wanted to step out and show Jesus that he was *getting it… at least sort of*. As we will see, he made a few crazy mistakes. By trying out his faith, Peter showed everyone, then and now, that Jesus welcomes our feeble efforts, forgives and rescues us when we falter, and affirms the faith we act on, no matter how small. Jesus is absolutely trustworthy. This week we'll examine Peter's first brave steps of faith.

Dear God, What would a big step of faith look like for me? How can I show you that I have learned something?
Do I have to prove my love for you? Or will taking these steps draw me closer to you?
Help me step out, Lord, and help me when I fall. Amen.

WEEK THREE, DAY ONE
READY TO STEP OUT

You can only learn so much in a classroom. Whether you're in middle school, high school, ski school, the school of rock, or the school of discipleship—eventually you have to step out into the real world and apply what you have learned. Ready or not, you have to take a step of faith. And often those first steps result in doubts, stumbles, or big mistakes.

Have you ever heard of dry land ski school? Growing up in Southern California, where snow is scarce, I attended a dry land ski school at my high school. We learned how to shuffle forward on skis, get up after a fall, side-step up hills, and point the skis down the mountain ... all on the grassy, treeless, slope-less high school football field! Reality hit home on Saturday, when we arrived at the snowy mountainside, ready to try out our new skills. As you might imagine, actual downhill skiing was more difficult than we expected. I felt confident until the moment I picked up a little speed ... and hit a tree. Navigating through trees on a real ski slope, wearing cumbersome equipment, unsure of my speed, I realized I still had much to learn.

ROCKIN' ON THE WATER

It happened after that incredible feeding miracle. The disciples were still analyzing what Jesus had done that afternoon. How could there have been twelve baskets left over from such a tiny sack lunch? After loading the disciples in the boat and sending them home, Jesus walked up the mountain alone. The disciples pulled hard at the oars to get back across the lake before the weather turned. But as the sun set, the wind whipped their sails. As the waves swelled, they remembered the time Jesus almost slept through a squall. Where was Jesus now? I imagine Peter and the others were praying for a quick end to this storm too. Suddenly, Jesus appears.

Read Matthew 14:22–25. What was Jesus doing? _____ Wait ... *what*?

Have you ever seen anyone do that? What would you think if you saw this? _____

Read the rest of the story in Matthew 14:26–33.

Naturally, the disciples thought they were seeing a ghost. It was almost impossible to see anything in the darkness, with the spray from the breaking waves in their faces, but Peter was "having a moment." He thought he recognized Jesus.

PETER. ROCK.

Let's clarify what Peter said to Jesus. Peter said which of the following:
- ❏ "Hey, what's the password?"
- ❏ "How *did* you feed all those people?"
- ❏ "When you said we would be fishers of men, we didn't think you meant we would be fishing them out of the lake."
- ❏ "Tell me to come to you."

Peter wasn't joking. He recognized Jesus in the middle of a crisis and wanted to be with him. Do you think Peter really believed he could walk on water? _____ yes _____ maybe _____ no

Why do you think he had the guts to try? _____

_____

CHEW ON THIS: *Stop for a minute and ask yourself, "Would I have the courage to step out of the boat, onto the water?" If Jesus told you to do it, would you attempt something you believed was impossible?*

At the moment Peter steps out of the boat, he gives us an example of the courage that comes from trust in Jesus.

Then what happened to Peter?
- ❏ He danced right up to Jesus, "Ta da!"
- ❏ He encouraged the others to try it too.
- ❏ He saw the wind and said, "No problem. This is fun!"
- ❏ He took a few steps, got scared, and started to sink.
- ❏ He screamed, "Lord, save me!"

CHEW ON THIS: *Stop again and ask yourself, "If I was failing at the very thing God had asked me to do, would I be willing to ask him to save me?"*

Lord, Save Me! by Norwegian artist, Mons Breidvik, 1921

When Peter looks away from Jesus and starts to sink, he demonstrates our very human condition—our tendency to focus on the crisis instead of the Christ. When Peter called for help, Jesus responded. Fortunately, Jesus was there to catch Peter and lift him up, saving him from drowning.

Remember, Jesus is always there, willing to pick you up from your failures and ready to hold your hand as you learn and grow.

Once everyone was together again in the boat, the winds died down. It's great to have Jesus in your boat. The disciples, especially Peter, wondered how Jesus could have this much power. But even while wondering about that, Peter was more sure than ever of Jesus's love and concern for him. It took a lot of trust to step out of that boat during the storm.

So let's review. What was Peter's first big step of faith? _____

_____

CHEW ON THIS: *Is Jesus asking you to step into a difficult place, to do something really hard, so you can see his power? What might that be? Can you trust him enough to get out of your boat?*

PETER. ROCK.

WEEK THREE, DAY TWO
"WHO DO MEN SAY THAT I AM?"

That water-walking experience was a really big step for Peter. No more would he be just one of the guys. He wasn't just hangin' with the group anymore. Something had changed. Peter grew bold, more confident. He trusted his friend Jesus with his very life. The risks of following Jesus seemed worth it. The adventures along the road were amazing, exhilarating. Then a day came when Peter uttered something he would never forget.

Jesus and the disciples had traveled north of Capernaum, away from the shores of Lake Galilee to the region of Caesarea Philippi. They made their way to the foot of Mt. Hermon in the high, snow-capped mountains on the modern Syrian-Lebanese border. Most residents in this area were non-Jews, so the crowds following Jesus were thinner. Jesus took time to pray by himself. When he rejoined the disciples, he asked them a question.

Read Matthew 16:13–14. What question did Jesus ask? _____

The disciples had heard many of the things people were saying about Jesus. Who did the people guess He might be? _____

_____

His question was a good one, because everyone who had seen or heard Jesus was arguing about who Jesus was and where he got his authority and power. There had been one time in Nazareth when people claimed that Jesus was just the local carpenter's son (Matt. 13:53–58). Having seen Jesus as a little boy running around his father's workshop, they thought he was just another boy from Nazareth. The Pharisees even suggested he was connected with Beelzebub, the prince of demons (Matt. 12:24).

But the disciples had seen Jesus *heal* people—lepers, blind and deaf people, paralyzed people, people out of their minds with demons—he *even* brought that little girl back to life. He taught with such unusual authority and showed such gentle compassion. He even commanded the winds to be still. People were either awed or angered by Jesus.

Many years later, a Pharisee named Paul believed that Jesus was just a Jewish troublemaker, certainly not the Son of God, and for a while he zealously tried to destroy the early Christians. But then one day Paul met Jesus. You can read that story in Acts 9. It was a life-changing moment for Paul. And from that point on, Paul became the most outspoken Christian evangelist of all time.

CHEW ON THIS: *It is an important question. Who do you say Jesus is?* _____

_____

Peter liked to speak up. Sometimes he blurted out things he would later regret. But this time, his heart was sure, and he could not keep quiet. What was Peter's answer in Matthew 16:15–16?

_____

Peter's answer was amazing. Jesus was pleased. According to Jesus, how did Peter know this (verse 17)?

_____

The Holy Spirit still works that way. Can you think of something you know but can't fully explain?

_____

✝ CHRISTIAN REALITY CHALLENGE: *Write a sentence that states your current belief about who Jesus is. Be honest.* _____

_____

_____

On a scale of one to ten (ten is strongest) how strongly do you believe this?

_____

Is there a song on this week's playlist that says what you feel about who Jesus is?

_____

PETER. ROCK.

WEEK THREE, DAY THREE
A ROCK YOU CAN BUILD ON

The next thing Jesus said made Peter feel really, really good. First, Jesus declared Simon's name change was now official. He would be called Peter, which means *rock* in Greek. You may have heard the word petrified, like *petrified* wood. When a log or branch is buried for eons, percolating ground water carrying minerals gradually replaces the wood with stone, and it becomes petrified or rock-ified.

Jesus talked about solid foundations once in Matthew 7:24–25. What did he say?

_____

Read Matthew 16:17–19. What else did Jesus say in this passage?
- ❏ "Peter, you passed the big test! Now you can relax."
- ❏ "I'm going to build my church on this rock, this Peter-rock."
- ❏ "You're going to Hollywood!"
- ❏ "The gates of Hades (Hell) will not overcome this church."
- ❏ "I give you the keys to the kingdom of Heaven."

Score. Peter was stunned. Jesus was going to use him to build his church? What could that mean? Can you imagine Peter's joy and excitement? He must be doing something right.

This was Peter's second big step of faith: declaring his complete faith in Jesus as the Messiah, the Son of God.

GET BEHIND ME!

While Peter was still feeling really good about himself and his new rock-solid name, Jesus started talking about going to Jerusalem. He promised there would be trouble with the religious leaders. He mentioned suffering. He even said he must be *killed*.

Read Matthew 16:21–28.

Peter was shocked. Things were going well, he thought. With people coming to Jesus in droves, his popularity had grown. No one could imagine anything but more miracles, more good times, maybe even deliverance from the oppressive Roman government. Peter's faith statement built up the disciples' hope that Jesus really was the promised Messiah, who would restore the kingdom of Israel. They even began dreaming of the fame and influence they might gain by hanging around as close FOJs (Friends of Jesus.) So, what's this about Jesus being *killed*?

Have you ever been so startled by what someone is saying that you don't even hear the rest of the sentence? _____

What additional thing did Jesus mention at the end Matthew 16:21? _____

_____

Do you think Peter heard that last part? Before he took time to think, Peter pulled Jesus aside and said, *"Never, Lord!"* Why would Peter say this?

Below are some possibilities, but what do you think? _____
- ❏ He counted Jesus as his best friend and didn't want anything to happen to him.
- ❏ He didn't think it made any sense for the Son of God to be killed.
- ❏ He didn't fully understand the purpose of Jesus's coming.
- ❏ He wanted to become famous with Jesus.
- ❏ He figured if Jesus was going to be killed, he would be too, and he was ready to fight.

At that point, while speaking to Peter, Jesus rebuked Satan. Yikes! Suddenly, Peter is not so smart. Jesus corrected him, even referring to Peter as Satan. Even so, Jesus continued to love Peter.

Poor Peter. He must have felt that following Jesus was a very rough road. One minute you think you truly understand him, trust him … the next, you realize you are still very confused. Two steps forward and one step back. Would he ever learn how to be a true believer? How could he ever live up to Jesus' expectations of him as "the rock?"

CHEW ON THIS: *How does it feel when you find you have completely misunderstood something important? What do you usually do when that happens?*

PETER. ROCK.

WEEK THREE, DAY FOUR
WHITE LIGHTNING

About a week later, while they were still in the mountains, Jesus took Peter, James, and John up to a high point for some small-group prayer time. While they were up on that peak, something unforgettable happened. The incident is recorded in three gospels—Matthew, Mark, and Luke—each with unique details.

WHY FOUR GOSPELS?

The four accounts of Jesus' life give us different perspectives and different details on many events. Multiple reports give the life of Jesus more credibility and color. The personality and purpose of each author differs slightly, yet the "good news" is the same in all four.

Matthew, Mark, and Luke, known as the synoptic gospels, are very similar, almost word-for-word copies. John is unique in style and covers many stories the others omit.

Matthew:
Author – the disciple Matthew (Levi, the tax collector)
Purpose – to prove that Jesus was the Messiah and that he fulfilled Old Testament scriptures. Matthew has the most Old Testament quotations.

Mark:
Author – Mark, a close friend of Peter
Purpose – A short, fast-paced, and vivid account of Jesus's ministry. No Christmas story is included.

Luke:
Author – the Gentile doctor Luke, who also wrote Acts.
Purpose – Luke records more parables, more prayer references, and a Christmas story complete with angels and shepherds.

John:
Author – the disciple John
Purpose – to prove Jesus is the Son of God. The "I AM" sayings, much poetic imagery, and, of course, the well-known John 3:16, make John's gospel unique.

The Transfiguration event is recounted in the first three gospels. Read it first in Matthew 17:1–9 and keep a bookmark there in your Bible. We will be reading verses from the other gospels to fill in extra details.

According to Luke 9:28, why did they go up the mountain? _____

That's important. Prayer opens the door for us to see God's glory, his purpose, his love, his guidance.

PETER: ROCK STAR FROM GALILEE

List all the words used to describe the face and clothing of Jesus from the three gospel accounts.

	face	clothing
Matthew 17:2	_____	_____
Mark 9:3	_____	_____
Luke 9:29	_____	_____

Which description really captures your imagination? _____

I love the sizzling, electric flash of lightning metaphor, because I have seen a single flash of lightning light up even the darkest night. And the thing about lightning is it happens so fast. If you blink, you miss it.

Suddenly, two people appeared with Jesus. Who were they?
_____ and _____

What do you know about these two characters from the Old Testament? _____
_____

You probably remember Moses was the one who parted the Red Sea (Ex. 14:13–31) and brought the Ten Commandments down from Mount Sinai (Ex. 20). Elijah was a prophet during the reign of the bad King Ahab (1Kings 17–19). Remember, these guys had been dead for hundreds of years.

What might they have talked about? _____
_____

Do you think Jesus called them by name? _____ If he did, what would that tell you about Jesus?
_____

What does Luke 9:30–31 tell us about the conversation? _____
_____

Wow. The Greek word for departure is *exodus*. In the Old Testament, the deliverance of God's people from bondage in Egypt was known as the Exodus. Just as Moses led the people into freedom from human bondage, Jesus would soon lead believers into spiritual freedom from sin. Jesus was going to die in Jerusalem and be raised to life, but his "departure" would be only the beginning.

If you were Peter, what would be going through your mind when this lightning-lit conversation was going on? _____
_____

PETER. ROCK.

WEEK THREE, DAY FIVE
ON THE MOUNTAIN WITH THE KING OF GLORY

The Transfiguration, by Danish realist,
Carl Heinrich Bloch (1834-1890)

This is how I imagine the Transfiguration:

Peter, James, and John are admiring the view from the mountaintop, perhaps discussing recent events, maybe arguing over who was the best disciple. Suddenly, they hear voices. Jesus is talking to someone, and when they turn, they see three awesome, glowing figures. The visitors wear robes like the prophets of old. The two men seem to know Jesus, and when he calls them by name, the disciples understand they are Moses and Elijah. Frightened by the sight of these living figures, Peter, James, and John fall face down on the ground.

Trembling, not knowing what to say, Peter bellows, "It's a good thing we're here, Lord, so we can build ... something. How about a shelter, maybe one for each of you?"

While Peter blurts out his half-baked plan to build shelters, a cloud settles on all of them. Peter is terrified.

James and John are stunned speechless. Then a mist covers everything, and a voice like thunder scares them even more. Before they can think another thought, it's over. Jesus alone is standing before them saying, "Don't be afraid; get up."

Read Mark 9:5–6. Peter's suggestion to build three shelters was:
- ❑ Helpful, since it was cloudy and looked like rain.
- ❑ An offer to do something to make this more permanent.
- ❑ An indication that Peter thought the kingdom of Heaven had arrived.
- ❑ A desperate attempt to say the right thing, to show that he revered all three people.

Then a voice boomed out. What four things were said (Matt. 17:5)?

_____

_____

It had to be the voice of God. Peter and the others had surely heard about the voice at Jesus' baptism a couple of years before. Funny, this mountain-top voice was saying the same things—almost.

PETER: ROCK STAR FROM GALILEE

Read Mark 1:10–11 and compare it to Matthew 17:5. What was different this time?

_____

_____

"Listen to him!" Pay attention. Not only is Jesus who you think he is, but everything he says is true. Everything he says should ring in your ears. He is eternally more important than the law (Moses) or the prophets (Elijah). And not only are you witnessing his earthly ministry, Peter, but this awesome, shining brightness you see today is what heavenly glory is like. "Listen to him!"

It was a big moment, a terrifying moment for Peter. Fortunately, in spite of his suggestion to build shelters, Jesus simply said, "Get up. Don't be afraid." In the coming months, Peter would still put his foot in his mouth many times. But he hung on to this truth: Jesus is the Son of God. After all, he actually heard God say, *"Listen to him!"* Those three disciples never forgot the awesome glory they saw that day. Many years later, both John and Peter commented on this experience. (See John 1:14 and 2 Peter 1:16–18.)

CHEW ON THIS: *Do you take time to listen to Jesus? How can you to listen to Jesus today?*

CHRISTIAN REALITY CHALLENGE: *Listen for what Jesus is saying to you. If you can, tell your group or a mentor about it.*

REVIEW

Recall all the steps Peter took in this week's lesson. Mark a B next to those you think were a step backward, and an F (forward) beside those you think were a step in the right direction.
- ❏ recognizing Jesus in the storm
- ❏ getting out of the boat
- ❏ keeping eyes on Jesus, taking a step
- ❏ watching the wind and waves
- ❏ declaring that Jesus is the Christ, the Son of the living God
- ❏ suggesting that Jesus will never have to die
- ❏ offering to build shelters for Jesus, Moses, and Elijah

What do all the B steps have in common? _____

What do all the F steps have in common? _____

CHEW ON THIS: *Do you think it is possible to avoid all backward steps in your faith journey? If so, how would you do it?* _____

If not, why not? _____

Are you ready to take some steps of faith?

WEEK THREE: INTO MY LIFE

Am I willing to take big (or little) steps of faith?

JAM SESSION

- Even if Jesus told you to do it, would you attempt something you believed was impossible, like walking on water?

- If you were failing at the very thing God asked you to do, would you ask him to save you? What would it take for you to ask for help?

- Who do *you* say Jesus is? Many religions recognize Jesus as a historical figure. Some think of him as a good moral teacher, but not God. Some consider him a prophet, but not the Son of God. What kind of sentence did you write about your current belief in Jesus? What questions do you still have about him? Can you go forward in faith even with questions?

- What do you do if you don't understand something in the Bible?

- How do you listen to Jesus today? Do you treat your Bible like your cell phone?

- Is it possible to avoid backward steps in your faith journey?

- Why don't people get "out of the boat" and come to Jesus in the middle of life's storms? What is it that intimidates us?

- Which song on the playlist do you most relate to? Why?

✝ CHRISTIAN REALITY CHALLENGES

Step out of the boat.

Listen to what Jesus is saying to you.

↩ WEEK THREE REPLAY

It is likely that we will make mistakes as we step out in faith, just like Peter did. So what are we afraid of? Think of the exciting water-walking possibilities of faith in Jesus. Isn't it worth it? Can you make a resolution to choose the path of faith even when it seems risky? In the 2009 Disney nature movie, *Earth*, a memorable scene shows a baby bird taking its first step out of the nest. The bird falls to the ground, happily landing in a soft pile of leaves. It's hard to fly, but you only learn if you take that first step out of the nest. Remember that Jesus is always there to lift you up when you fall.

Dear Lord, I believe you are who you say you are.
I want to listen to you and move forward in faith.
I want to step out of the boat, but I know I will make mistakes,
so I trust you to be there to help me.
Thank you, Jesus. Amen.

WEEK FOUR

ROCK STAR WANNABE ON A ROCKY ROAD TRIP

But Peter insisted emphatically, "Even if I have to die with you, I will never disown you."
—Mark 14:31

PLAYLIST

Rock Star – Third Day
Let the Little Children Come to Me – June Armstrong
I Left Everything to Follow You – Michael Card
Your Kindness – Leslie Phillips
Let Us Break Bread Together – Spiritual
How Beautiful – Twila Paris
Remembrance – Matt Redman
The Servant Song – Richard Gilliard

WEEK FOUR PREVIEW

Ever wonder about the life of a rock band groupie? You know, the kind that knows the words of every song, doesn't miss a concert, wears the same hairstyle and clothes as the lead singer? These people are proud of their closeness to the star, but they are not stars themselves. They loudly defend anything their hero does, but if push came to shove they would probably run to save themselves.

In our study last week, Jesus dropped the bomb about his own certain death. But nobody wanted that to happen. The disciples couldn't imagine what would happen to them if Jesus died, so they put it out of their minds. How do you feel when someone predicts doom and gloom? In many cases you can't do a thing about it, so you just try to forget it. What if someone predicts you will do something awful, something you would never want to do. Do you think maybe they are crazy?

This week we follow Jesus and the disciples as they walk from Galilee to Jerusalem with the gathering flock of groupies wanting to be near Jesus. On the eve of Passover, the twelve will climb the steps to the upper room and eat their last meal together. At that dinner, Jesus predicts Peter's future.

Dear Lord, Help me to grow closer to you. There is much I do not understand, but I do want to be a good disciple. Open my eyes to the people around me that you want to love, and make me aware of my own pride and broken promises. Have I repented of my sins? Amen.

WEEK FOUR, DAY ONE
THE NINE-HUNDRED-POUND GORILLA IN THE ROOM

The disciples didn't really know how to react when Jesus laid out his depressing future. Jesus called Peter "Satan" back in Matthew 16, after he showed his undying support by declaring Jesus would never be killed. Let's see how the disciples responded the next time Jesus brought it up.

In Matthew 17:22–23 (NIV), what were the disciples filled with?

❏ joy ❏ indifference ❏ excitement ❏ grief

Other Bible translations say they were greatly distressed, very sad, or exceedingly sorry. In short, they felt terrible.

HIDE THE KIDS! CAN'T YOU SEE JESUS IS BUSY?

Convinced of Jesus' cosmic importance, the disciples couldn't let their grief distract them. Throngs of people pressed upon them everywhere they went. Crowd control became one of their main jobs. At one point, the crowd was crawling with kids like a Chuck E. Cheese pizza parlor on a Saturday afternoon.

Read Luke 18:15–17. What did the disciples do to "help" Jesus? _____

Oops. They got it wrong again. Jesus overruled them saying, "Let the _____ come to me, do not _____, for to such belongs the _____."

Jesus wanted to talk directly to the kids? That was amazing. Important people didn't waste time on street kids. Children counted for next to nothing. Rarely did an adult outside the family even speak to a child, but Jesus did.

Read the story again in Mark 10:13–16. How did Jesus feel about the disciples' actions?

_____

What does it tell you about Jesus, that he would take children in his arms and bless them?

_____

✝ **CHRISTIAN REALITY CHALLENGE:** *Hug your younger brother or sister today. Surprise a child with your kindness. It can be a small thing, but do it with love. Maybe you need to pray about it first. Try it again tomorrow. How does it feel?*

WEEK FOUR, DAY TWO
A SMALL MAN GETS A BIG HEART

Zachaeus, by Danish artist, Niels Larsen Stevns (1834-1890)

On the way to Jerusalem, Jesus repeated exactly what he knew would happen there. He mentioned it several times. What did he say in Luke 18:31–33? And according to Luke 18:34, how well did the disciples understand? _____

That nine-hundred-pound gorilla was still hanging around.

If your parents are like most American adults, they don't love filing tax returns. The IRS is subject to strict laws and the US tax code is complicated, yet no one can tax you double and keep the change. In Jesus's day, tax collectors had to turn over a set amount to the Roman government but were allowed to keep any extra they managed to collect. That meant tax collectors like Zaccheus could become very wealthy. All they needed was some convincing deception to force unsuspecting citizens to overpay.

Now, in the third year of Jesus's ministry, news of him had spread everywhere. When Zaccheus heard Jesus was coming to Jericho, like everyone else he was curious. So he raced to catch up to the clamoring mob.

Read Luke 19:1–9. Why did Zaccheus climb the tree? _____

As Jesus approached the tree with Zack in it, what do you think the disciples were thinking?
- ❏ Unbelievable. How did he get up there?
- ❏ Remembering the hole-in-the-roof entrance of the paralyzed man, they thought this guy needed some attention.
- ❏ Not surprised at all. Lately, people were hanging out of trees like monkeys everywhere they went.

I bet the whole crowd looked up when Jesus spotted the little man on a branch overhead. I can hear the locals whispering, "That's Zaccheus! He took my family's last denarius last month for taxes; I hate that guy."

ROCK STAR WANNABE ON A ROCKY ROAD TRIP

Why do you think Jesus suddenly invited himself over to this stranger's home?
- ❑ He was hungry.
- ❑ He knew it would shake up the town.
- ❑ He knew that if Zaccheus was curious enough to climb a tree, he was ready for an encounter with God.
- ❑ He liked short people.
- ❑ He did whatever the Father told him to do out of love.

The disciples overheard the locals muttering about Jesus eating with this dirty tax collector! Each had his own experience with tax collectors. In fact, one of them was a former tax collector himself. They were starting to expect this sort of thing from Jesus.

The encounter reminded them all that knowing Jesus changed people. Peter remembered how his life had changed when Jesus climbed into his boat long before. Zaccheus would be forever changed because Jesus came to his house. Led by the kindness of Jesus, Zaccheus repented, declaring he would pay back all he had taken from people, even up to four times what he owed them. A line from an old Leslie Phillips song says it this way: "It's your kindness that leads us to repentance, O Lord."

CHEW ON THIS: *Is it possible to become a Christian without repentance?*

Repentance is key. Whatever mistakes we make, God knows about them. And he loves us anyway. He comes to our house or our boat, and offers to be *with* us.

In verse 9, what did Jesus say had come to Zack's house? _____

Look up four of the following nine scriptures about salvation. Jot down what each one says, and comment on how they relate to the new Zaccheus.

Psalm 62 _____

Psalm 13:5 _____

Psalm 51:12 _____

Psalm 27:1 _____

Isaiah 12:1–3 _____

Romans 1:16–17 _____

2 Corinthians 7:10 _____

Ephesians 6:17 _____

1 Thessalonians 5:9 _____

Now, look up this outstanding verse and memorize it if you can: Acts 4:12. Write it here:

_____

_____

WEEK FOUR, DAY THREE
THE GORILLA... YET AGAIN

Yet again, Jesus describes the coming events in Jerusalem.

Read Mark 10:32–34. Any new reactions? _____
How many times did they have to hear this? Why so much repetition?

Can you remember a time when you had to be told something again and again before it finally sank in? _____

PASSOVER AT LAST

The Upper Room, Jerusalem

When Christmas is less than a week away, things get very busy at my house. There are parties to plan, gifts to buy and wrap, and special programs at church. I have to admit that sometimes the busyness of the season overshadows other things. I try to remember to pray and read my Bible, but other things get buried or forgotten. Does any of that happen at your house?

Peter and John were assigned the task of preparing a Passover Feast for Jesus and the crew. Read Luke 22:7–13. Jesus wanted a private room in Jerusalem for the meal. Since Jewish pilgrims from far and wide converged on Jerusalem every year for Passover, the city was packed. Peter and John located the guy with the water jug, obtained permission to have a feast at his house, and got busy with shopping and preparations. There was plenty to do. For one thing, they were required to present a lamb for sacrifice at the temple. Bitter herbs, *charoset* (a chunky paste of fruits and nuts), and plenty of wine would be needed too. While Peter and John walked the crowded streets, they recalled some of the amazing events of the week so far.

1. They had been pleasantly surprised as they entered Jerusalem a few days before. Jesus had insisted on riding a donkey down the hill from Bethany to Jerusalem (Matt. 21:1–11). Multitudes of palm-waving, cheering supporters appeared, and all Scripture-savvy Jews whispered about the donkey. They remembered Zechariah 9:9, which predicted the king coming to Jerusalem on a donkey. With all this hoopla, the disciples started believing Jesus was the long expected King. They hoped all his dire predictions would prove false.

   Read Luke 19:38–40. What did Jesus say would happen if the disciples kept quiet?

   _____

2. The disciples' giddiness at the triumphal entrance was quickly replaced by tension when Jesus knocked over the moneychangers' tables in the temple (Matt. 21:12–15). If Jesus was going to challenge the Pharisees and temple authorities like that, things might not go so well, after all. It was a good thing they were staying in Bethany at the house of Jesus' close friends Mary, Martha, and Lazarus.

3. And, oh, the stories Jesus had been using to illustrate his teaching in the temple courts all week! He told a parable about a vineyard owner who went on a long journey. The farmers who were to care for the vineyard rebelled, killing the owner's servants and eventually even the owner's son. The parable really upset the teachers of the law, because they understood Jesus was talking about them.

   Read Luke 20:9–19. What question did Jesus ask the teachers in verse 17?

   _____

   _____

   What do you think he was talking about? _____

4. And what about the expensive perfume Mary had poured over Jesus (John 12:1–8)? Talk about smelling like a rose… Judas had been upset about the wasted value. Did he really want to give the money to the poor? Or did he just want to skim some for himself?

   What did he say in John 12:7? _____

Yikes! There it was again, a reference to his own death, but they still couldn't understand.

> **CHEW ON THIS:** *"The poor you will always have with you." Is this statement still true today? Is Jesus saying that we can't do anything about poverty?*

PETER: ROCK STAR FROM GALILEE

WEEK FOUR, DAY FOUR
TIME TO EAT

The Last Supper, by Titian, Italian Renaissance artist
(1488-1576)

Peter and John were tired from jostling through the streets all day, hauling food and supplies to the upper room. They laid out the unleavened bread, wine, roast lamb, dipping oil, and all the bitter herbs that went with the meal. They set a special place for Jesus. At last, the meal was ready. Now, they could finally relax and reflect on the Passover story: how almighty God had delivered their ancestors from slavery in Egypt. The Passover rituals were familiar to all of them from years of faithful observance. Did the disciples have any way of knowing this would be their last meal together?

DIRTY FEET

Read John 13:1–20. The food smelled good; everyone was hungry. Suddenly, Jesus stood up, filled a basin with water, and began washing everyone's feet.

What was he doing? The rest of the guys accepted the foot washing without question. But Peter could not stand it. What might he have been thinking?

- ❏ Why can't we just eat supper? The food is getting cold.
- ❏ I could have done this; why didn't I think of it?
- ❏ I should have asked that household servant downstairs to do this for us.
- ❏ Something is wrong here. The Son of God should not have to wash my stinking feet.

Peter was indignant. This was something you had servants for. Then, after backing away, Peter flips 180 degrees and says, "OK, then wash all of me." Peter wanted so much to say and do the right things so he might outshine the other disciples. He had blundered so many times before, but he really wanted this night to be perfect.

CHEW ON THIS: *What kind of example was Jesus setting for the disciples? Why was this so important? What does it mean to you?*

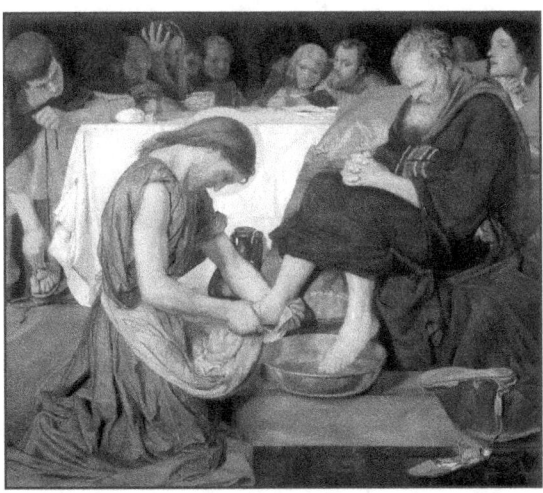

Christ Washing Saint Peter's Feet, by Ford Madox Brown (1821-1893). Notice Peter's expression of resignation.

CHRISTIAN REALITY CHALLENGE: *Do some unexpected service for somebody this week. It could be a family member, a friend, or even a stranger. You could offer to mow your neighbor's lawn, bake cookies for your school librarian, or clean the bathroom for your mom. Be creative. Share the experience with your study group.*

WEEK FOUR, DAY FIVE
THE FELLOWSHIP OF THE FEAST

I once had dinner at a Japanese restaurant where the tables were low, and we sat on the ground. A reclining meal, like the Last Passover, was similar.

> Read Luke 22:14–20. Jesus' words during the last supper were burned into the disciples' memory. First, he drank one cup of wine and asked them all to share it, because it would be His last. Then he took bread, gave thanks, and broke it. What did he say? (v. 19)

_____

_____

There were many other scripted remarks for the Passover feast. Luke has omitted them here. Jesus would have retold the story of the Exodus from Egypt, as the youngest in the group asked the Four Questions, beginning with "Why is this night different from all other nights? The central theme of this meal was freedom. The Exodus was God's deliverance of his people from their slavery to men. Jesus was about to deliver all people from their slavery to sin.

> After the meal, Jesus took another cup of wine. What did he say about it? (v. 20)

_____

_____

After all the events surrounding Jesus' death took place, this meal, especially these words related to the bread and wine, became the model for what we now call Communion, or Holy Eucharist. For Christians throughout the ages, the bread and wine are sacred symbols of Jesus' body and blood, shed for many for the forgiveness of sins. Praise be to God for this wonderful gift.

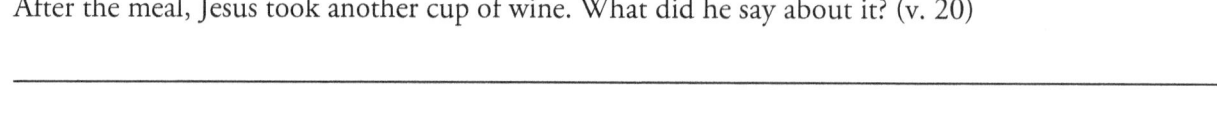 **CHRISTIAN REALITY CHALLENGE:** *The next time you take communion, remember this last supper Jesus had with his disciples. Remember the foot washing, Peter's brave promise, and the new command.*

The disciples sat speechless for a while after supper. The wine, the exhausting week, and the sad comments by Jesus had taken a toll.

What did Jesus tell them in Luke 22:21–22? _____

Alert again, they began bantering about who could possibly do that, and the recurring discussion of who was the greatest came up again. Read Luke 22:23–27. Don't you think the foot washing would have been fresh in their minds? Jesus seemed to know they had a rather short attention span.

PETER'S FUTURE UNVEILED

After all of this—the preparation, the unexpected foot-washing ceremony, the meal with added symbolism, the arguments—Peter was again filled with emotion. He had learned much from this good man, this Son of God, since that day by the Sea of Galilee when Jesus had asked him to follow. Peter loved Jesus and had every intention of following him to death. In fact, he was rather proud of how far he had come.

Read Luke 22:31–34. What would happen before the rooster crowed? _____

_____

CHEW ON THIS: *If your best friend told you that you were going to disown him/her, how would you respond?*

Peter insisted he would be faithful to the end. It is helpful to look at each gospel account of Peter's words. Read them now.

Matthew 26:33 _____

Mark 14:29 _____

Mark 14:31 _____

Luke 22:33 _____

John 13:37 _____

Summarize what Peter is trying to say: _____

_____

At this point, Peter is committed to being the best disciple. He is willing to defend Jesus to the death. Having been through some controversy with the authorities, Peter thought he was ready to fight if necessary. He was strong, and his bravado was even stronger. Following Jesus doesn't mean proudly promising what we may not be able to deliver. But Peter didn't know that yet.

A NEW COMMANDMENT

John's gospel preserves Jesus' words spoken after supper on the way to the garden. In John 15:9–17, Jesus issued a new commandment. What was it? _____
_____

Compared to the long list of commandments in the Old Testament, this one sounds so simple. Let me ask you this. Which do you find easier: loving God or loving other people? What kind of love is Jesus talking about here? Is it love for family, friends, and people who think like you? Is it love that goes out of the way to help? Is it love that involves sacrifice? I believe this kind of love is only possible when we really understand what Jesus did in going to the cross.

Jesus said, "As I have loved you, so you must love one another." How had Jesus loved them? Give some examples from what you know already. _____
_____
_____

What does it mean to you that Jesus loved you enough to die for you?
_____
_____
_____

CHEW ON THIS: *What kind of sacrifice would you be willing to make for someone you love?*

WEEK FOUR: INTO MY LIFE

Jesus wants me to follow him, but then he talks about dying. What's up with that?

JAM SESSION

- What new thing have you learned this week about Jesus?

- What song on the playlist best relates to what you learned?

- Is it possible to become a Christian without repentance?

- What did Jesus mean when he said, "The poor you will always have with you, but you will not always have me"?

- What kind of example was Jesus setting for the disciples when he washed their feet? Why was this so important? What does it mean to you?

- If your best friend told you that you were going to disown him/her, how would you respond?

- What does it mean to you that Jesus loved you enough to die for you?

- What kind of sacrifice would you be willing to make for someone you love?

CHRISTIAN REALITY CHALLENGES

Surprise a child with your kindness.

Do an unexpected service.

Remember the Last Supper during communion.

Give something up out of love.

 ### WEEK FOUR REPLAY

During their final trip to Jerusalem for Passover, each disciple's thoughts increasingly focused on who they understood Jesus to be. Peter, James, and John, convinced of Jesus's divinity, seemed bent on staying close; ready to defend him against any violence. Others became more and more confused whenever Jesus spoke. Judas Iscariot, the Zealot who was most eager to see Israel return to its former glory, may have considered how he might force Jesus into a power grab. Or he may have concluded that Jesus was not really the Messiah at all. He left dinner early, his plan well known by Jesus alone.

The Passover meal took on a whole new meaning with Jesus' words and actions. As the eleven weary disciples rose from dinner for their customary walk to Gethsemane for prayer, unresolved questions remained. They knew one thing for sure, though. Jesus counted them as his friends, and he loved them.

Dear Jesus, You know everything I have done. I think I know who you are, but I surely don't fully understand. Be patient with me when I fail to live up to my own promise to follow you. Thank you, Lord, for loving me no matter what. Amen.

WEEK FIVE

ROCKSLIDE

...the rooster crowed. The Lord turned and looked straight at Peter... He went outside and wept bitterly.
—Luke 22:60–62

PLAYLIST

Amazing Love – Chris Tomlin
Better Than a Hallelujah – Amy Grant
Before the Morning – Josh Wilson
What Wondrous Love Is This – Alexander Means
Call My Name – Third Day
You Are More – Tenth Avenue North

WEEK FIVE PREVIEW

The dinner is over; the drama begins. Peter makes his biggest blunders after boldly claiming he would die for Jesus. We look at the contrasting reactions of Judas and Peter to their own personal failures as disciples. Jesus loved them both, but only one remembered this in his dark hour. We will look closely at the cross and learn that Jesus knew exactly what was happening to him and why. As Jesus forgives even the men pounding stakes into his wrists, we remember how much God loves us. Finally, bewilderment turns to joy when Jesus appears alive to Peter and the rest, offering peace.

Dear Lord, In my efforts to please you, I often promise too much. Then I mess up.
Sometimes it leads me to feel hopeless, even desperate.
Forgive me and remind me that the morning of your resurrection is all
I need. Do you really love me that much? Amen.

WEEK FIVE, DAY ONE
TOO TIRED

Gethsemane at Night

Exhaustion. Complete exhaustion. The end of a long day. The end of a long race. Marathon runners collapse across the finish line, tennis champions fall to the ground after a grueling match, and college students crash after studying all night for an exam. Once in high school, while attempting to finish a book late one night, I fell asleep—with my eyes *open*! My parents found me slumped in bed with the light on, eyes wide open, but sound asleep. I was too tired to even realize that I was tired.

At the conclusion of supper in the upper room of a house somewhere in Jerusalem, Peter was understandably tired. He had worked hard preparing the Passover meal. Jesus had stretched their minds with his foot-washing demo and discussion. Tension had gripped everyone when Judas exited the room. Jesus had talked about going somewhere, about betrayal and death. Peter offered his unflagging support, but Jesus calmly told him that he would deny him. John 14–17 records the lengthy prayers and intimate discussion Jesus had with the eleven disciples after dinner. When you have some time, and you're not too tired ☺, read those chapters.

Then Jesus led them on a brisk walk through some dark streets, past the Temple, on a narrow trail down into the Kidron Valley, and up the Mount of Olives. They sat down in an olive grove called Gethsemane, which means oil press. Jesus asked Peter, James, and John to come a little farther, closer to Jesus' favorite prayer place. It was dark, cool, and breezy; everyone was exhausted.

Read Matthew 26:36–41. What did Jesus feel? _____

What did Peter and the others feel? _____

How long had Jesus been praying? _____ How would you be feeling at this point? _____

Continue reading Matthew 26:42–46. The quiet spring night was too comfortable. Jesus needed the prayer support of his friends, but they couldn't deliver.

What happened instead? _____

How do you feel about Peter right now?
- ❏ I understand; he's just tired.
- ❏ It seems like he could have stayed awake a little while.
- ❏ What's wrong with him? Didn't he hear what Jesus had said?

Exhaustion affects us all in different ways. How does it usually affect you?

_____

_____

CHEW ON THIS: *If your friend called or texted you in the middle of the night because he/she needed you to pray, could you do it?*

WEEK FIVE, DAY TWO
LIKE A NIGHTMARE

Suddenly, torchlight dances on the olive trees, soldiers' swords clank in their scabbards, and Judas appears. What's going on? Adrenaline surging, Peter shakes himself awake and leaps to his feet. No time to pray now.

Read Matthew 26:47–56 and John 18:1–11. What was Judas's predetermined signal? _____

Why did they need a signal? Didn't they know what Jesus looked like? These were soldiers and officers hired by the chief priests to arrest Jesus under cover of darkness. A guy named Malchus got a little too close to Peter. What happened to him? _____

According to John 18:10–11, who was responsible for this? _____

Are you surprised? Why or why not? _____

Peter made another error in judgment. Rather than chiding him, Jesus simply said, "Put your sword away! Shall I not drink the cup the Father has given me?"

Jesus displayed incredible calmness during his arrest. His hour of prayer gave him strength for this humiliating arrest. Compare Peter's fighting reflex with Jesus' calm acceptance.

What factors led Jesus to be calm while Peter reacted violently? _____

CHEW ON THIS: *When you are up against a real test of your character, how do you handle the pressure? What are some practical things you could do to have more peace in those situations?*

_____

As the soldiers cuffed Jesus, the disciples fled. Their fears consumed them, and many stayed under cover until the next week. Peter felt badly that he failed Jesus by sleeping instead of praying and then again by striking Malchus, so he followed at a distance, hoping something would happen to turn things around.

When the posse of soldiers arrived at the high priest's house, Peter joined a group of servants and bystanders awakened by the noisy street procession. By this time, it might have been after midnight and getting chilly.

Read Luke 22:54–62. To warm up a bit, what did they do in the courtyard? _____

ROCKSLIDE

Imagine the faces lit up around the crackling fire, the hushed gossip about what was happening. Imagine Peter, asking a few questions about the proceedings, hoping against hope that he might be able to *do* something to help Jesus. But his voice and accent gave him away.

What did they accuse Peter of? _____

In the three short verses of Luke 22:60–62, Peter's emotions take radical turns.

What is his outward emotion in verse 60? _____

What do you think he's feeling to cause that outburst? _____

Then, the rude awakening of the rooster crowing and *the look*: Jesus turning to find Peter in the crowd. How does Peter feel now? _____

Remembering Jesus's prediction after supper in the upper room just hours before (it seemed like ages ago), his heart sinks. He's done it—the unthinkable. The thing he never thought he would do. He has denied his Lord, his best friend.

Now what is his outward emotion? _____ Why is he feeling this? _____

It all happened so fast. From foot washing to hand wringing, from food and wine to dreadful drowsiness, from overconfidence to despair; a very foggy Friday was about to dawn.

CHEW ON THIS: *Have you ever said something you didn't want to say, lied to protect yourself, and regretted your comments almost immediately? When?*

WEEK FIVE, DAY THREE
CRYING THE BLUES

Conscience: Judas, by Russian realist, Nicolai Ge (1831-1894)
Notice the other disciples in the distance.

It was Friday. Ironically, Christians now call it Good Friday, but none of the disciples considered it good at the time. Friday was a tough day for all of them, but for Judas Iscariot and Simon Peter, it was about the worst day of their lives. Compared to what we know about Peter, Judas is a complete stranger. He's like the guy who goes on a shooting spree, and when his neighbors find out they say, "He *seemed* like a nice person."

It is interesting to compare Peter and Judas. Both answered the call to follow Jesus. They traveled together. They saw all the same miracles, heard the same gentle teachings, and witnessed the tension with the authorities. They went to the same school: the school of discipleship. Jesus loved them both.

We know Peter was one of the three closest to Jesus; he was included in some of the most important events. He asked tons of questions; he made a great statement of faith, even trusted Jesus enough to take a few steps on the stormy sea.

We don't know as much about Judas. Was he a loner? Did he lag behind all the time? Why was he following Jesus at all? Did he really understand Jesus? Did he really *know* Jesus? Did he just misunderstand Jesus's mission?

> Read John 12:1–8. What is the main thing we learn about Judas from this passage?
> ❑ He was in agreement with the others.
> ❑ He wanted to take care of the poor.
> ❑ He was a thief.
> ❑ He liked to debate fine points about charity.

There are no other references to this disciple outside of his actions on this fateful Thursday and Friday.

> What did Judas do on Thursday night? Read John 13:26–30 and Matthew 26:47–50. Why do you think he did that? _____

> Read Mathew 27:3–5. What did he do on Friday morning with the coins he got Thursday night?
> _____

What was he thinking now? _____

Then his despair got the best of him. We know he was sorry, but for some reason, he felt there was only one thing for him to do. Have you ever known anyone who was this desperate?

CHEW ON THIS: *How do people get suicidal? Is suicide ever a good option? Can you tell when someone is depressed and perhaps desperate? What can you do about it?*

Peter was depressed too. Why? What had he done? _____

Judas's betrayal led to Jesus' arrest and ultimate death, but didn't Peter essentially betray Jesus too? Didn't he claim to not even know Jesus, when in fact they were the closest of friends? And now it seemed there was no way to make it right. Peter knew who Jesus was—the Son of God. Peter had failed Jesus before, and each time Jesus had forgiven him. But this was the worst.

We don't know what Peter did all day. We don't know where he went to hide. He may have felt as desperate as Judas, but he did not take his own life.

CHEW ON THIS: *What do you think was the difference between Peter and Judas? Why did they act so differently in the face of personal failure, grief, and remorse? Could it be that only one of them knew that Jesus loved him? Peter had tested that relationship time and again. He had tried and failed; he had been forgiven. Do you think Judas just never got close enough to learn how much Jesus loved him?*

CHEW ON THIS: *If you made a mistake of huge proportions, or if you were so depressed and desperate that you wondered if you could go on, who would you most relate to, Peter or Judas?*

CHRISTIAN REALITY CHALLENGE: *If you see a very sad person at school, or even in your church group, what can you do to help that person know for certain that Jesus loves them? It's hard to know what to say to someone like that. But pray about it. Ask God to give you the words or the gestures that might make a difference. Maybe someone else could help—like a teacher or pastor or parent. Should you tell someone what you noticed? Pray about it.*

Depression is very real, and it has many causes. But you can always know that Jesus loves you and that he is with you and understands how you feel. Even if you don't feel like he loves you, that doesn't mean that he doesn't. We don't really feel gravity until we trip, but gravity is always working. Jesus will never let you go. Get to know him through prayer and Bible reading. Tell him why you feel depressed. Know that he is listening.

Always remember this: Jesus LOVES you!!!!!

WEEK FIVE, DAY FOUR
THREE DAYS THAT CHANGED THE WORLD

FRIDAY: LOVE SO AMAZING, SO DIVINE

So, Peter is having a breakdown and Judas is suicidal while Jesus is being falsely accused, ridiculed, and tortured. Let's walk with Jesus through the next twenty hours, beginning at the home of Caiphas, the high priest.

JESUS' LAST HOURS

Here is a handy reference to the four gospel accounts of Jesus' death and resurrection.

	On Trial	Crucifixion	Death	Burial	Resurrection
Matthew 27	v.1–2, 11–31	v. 32–44	v. 45–56	v. 57– 66	Chapter 28
	Barabbas pardoned	Jesus quotes Ps. 22		Joseph rolls stone	
Mark 15	v.1–20	v. 21–32	v. 33–41	v. 42–47	Chapter 16
Luke 23	v. 1–25	v. 26–43	v. 44–49	v. 50–56	Chapter 24
	Pilate's wife's dream		Jesus forgives thief		Road to Emmaus
John 18	v. 28 to 19:16	19: 17–29	19: 30–37	19: 38–42	Chapter 20
		Jesus speaks to John and his mother			

St. Peter in Gallicantu Church, Jerusalem

Today there is a beautiful church built over the house of the high priest. It's called St. Peter in Gallicantu, which is Latin for 'cock-crow.'

Good Friday, Jesus in Prison, by French neoclassical artist,
James Tissot (1836-1902)

I once visited the dark cell in which they say Jesus was held. I cried. He was jailed by Jerusalem's religious elite, just a stone's throw from the Temple where God himself met with his people in the Holy of Holies. The leaders of God's people had God's Son in chains. Did they know how much he loved them? Sadly, no.

Read Luke 22:63–71 and Matthew 26:65–68. What time was it when the Sanhedrin (council of elders) began the "official" trial of Jesus? _____

What did Jesus say that made him "guilty?" _____

They found him guilty of blasphemy—claiming to be God. Convicted of speaking the truth, Jesus was bound again and marched across town to Pilate's Jerusalem palace. Pilate, the Roman governor of Judea (most of present-day Israel) was headquartered in Caesarea, about fifty miles away on the Mediterranean coast. He had come to Jerusalem at Passover in case there was unexpected trouble. These were dangerous times.

Read Mark 15:1–25. Did Pilate want to condemn Jesus, or do you think he wanted to release him?

_____

Why did he release Barabbas? (v. 24) _____

Antonia Fortress, Jerusalem

Jesus was flogged in the Antonia Fortress, the outpost of the Roman soldiers adjacent to the temple. Then, with his back stinging, bleeding, and swollen, he was forced to carry his cross along the city streets, now called the Via Dolorosa, the Way of Suffering. Thankfully, someone took the load of the cross and carried it for him most of the way.

Who was that man? (Luke 23: 26-31) _____

Perhaps as early as 9:00 A.M. (the third hour according to Mark 15:25) but no later than noon (the sixth hour according to Luke 23:44) Jesus was nailed, literally. He was lifted up.

According to Luke 23:32–34, what did he say? _____

_____

Can you believe it? Even while in the most horrible pain, both physical and emotional, Jesus knew the reason for his death: forgiveness. The sacrifice of his sinless, perfect life paid for the sins of the whole world, so that anyone, anywhere, at any time could be made holy, reconciled to God. The payment for sin has been made through Jesus Christ's blood.

Read the following verses: Matthew 26:28, Acts 10:43, Acts 13:38, Ephesians 1:7, and Hebrews 10:10. What message do you get from them? _____

_____

Now read Psalm 130. How does this speak to you? _____

The righteous King of the Universe allowed his only begotten Son to be slain for the sole purpose of obtaining our freedom from sin and its punishment. That is unfailing, amazing love! What wondrous love is this, oh my soul!

Darkness covered the area from noon to three, and during this time Jesus felt the suffocation that accompanied death by crucifixion. He said very little because of his dry mouth and thirst and, of course, the excruciating pain. But his mind was sharp, and he remembered Psalm 22:1. He started to recite it but could not even finish the first verse. Read this Psalm, the most quoted of all the Psalms in the New Testament. Then read Mark 15:33–37.

In what ways did Psalm 22 foreshadow what actually happened? _____

_____

So Jesus died. The earth shook, the sun hid, the temple veil was ripped from top to bottom, tombs opened, and dead people walked the streets (Matt. 27:51–53). Where was Peter? It was only about three o'clock in the afternoon. Yesterday at this time, Peter was still rushing around getting supper ready. We know of only one of the twelve who actually watched at the foot of the cross. That was John. But surely Peter knew what was happening. Everyone must have felt the earthquake.

What did the centurion say after witnessing the entire gruesome day (Matt. 27:54)?

_____

Now, since the Sabbath begins at sundown, there was little time in which to bury the body. Read John 19:38–42.

What two men took Jesus' body to the garden tomb? _____

And, in keeping with Jewish burial customs, what did they do to the body?

_____

I find it interesting that myrrh was a gift to the baby Jesus in the manger and it was used in Jesus's burial. It sort of completes the circle, no?

CHEW ON THIS: *What does Jesus' death mean to you personally?*

WEEK FIVE, DAY FIVE
THE REST OF THE STORY

SATURDAY: THE BLACKEST SABBATH

Sabbath began at sunset. It had been dark since noon. Jesus was dead. Hope was dead too. Everyone who thought Jesus would be the strong, new, mighty king of Israel—the one who could put them back on the map, so to speak—was now crushed. Pilate, still afraid that trouble might flare up, sent men to guard and secure the tomb (Matt. 27:65–66).

The faithful women—those who watched even as Jesus was crucified—had followed Joseph and Nicodemus to the garden tomb. They saw how the body was laid there.

> Read Luke 23:55–56. What did the women do just before and during the Sabbath?

CHRISTIAN REALITY CHALLENGE: *To simulate the sadness experienced by the disciples that day, try going without music of any kind for a whole day. No iPod, no radio, no tunes. You might want to partner with a friend when you try this. It's harder than you think.*

SUNDAY: THE MORNING MOST BRIGHT

Garden Tomb outside Jerusalem

We may grieve, cry ourselves to sleep, feel helpless, hopeless, or desperate at night, but things always seem a little better in the morning. The women who had witnessed the crucifixion set out for the garden before dawn, eager to anoint the body.

Read the following three gospel accounts of the morning and underline Peter's name wherever you see it: Matthew 28:1–10, Luke 24:1–12, and John 20:1–9.

Which account gives the most information about Peter? _____

Both Luke and John give details about Peter's visit to the tomb. What term best describes Peter at this point?   ❑ ecstatic   ❑ afraid   ❑ still depressed   ❑ confused

At first, Peter didn't get it. But I bet he called the disciples together so he could tell them what he had seen. Read John 20:10–20. When Jesus joined the group as they huddled behind locked doors, he spoke to them saying, "Peace be with you." (John 20:19) They were overjoyed.

That's cool, partly because they needed some serious stress relief, and partly because Jesus had predicted it. Read John 16:20–22. It happened just like Jesus said it would. Their sorrow became joy. They didn't know what the future held for them, but the fact of Jesus *alive* was enough to make them want to sing.

WEEK FIVE: INTO MY LIFE

Does Jesus really love me that much?

Note to Leaders: A 2009 movie, *To Save a Life*, (Rated PG-13) directed by Brian Baugh, written by Jim Britts, addresses some of the issues raised in this chapter. You might want to preview the movie and consider sharing it with your group.

JAM SESSION

- If your friend called or texted you in the middle of the night because he/she needed you to pray, could you do it? How does exhaustion usually affect you?

- When you are up against a real test of your character, how do you handle the pressure? What are some practical things you could do to have more peace in those situations?

- Have you ever done what Peter did: said something you didn't want to say, lied to protect yourself, or regretted your comments almost immediately?

- How do people get suicidal? Can you tell when someone is depressed and perhaps desperate? What can you do about it?

- What do you think was the difference between Peter and Judas? Why did they act so differently in the face of personal failure, grief, and remorse?

- What does Jesus' death mean to you personally?

- Choose one of the songs from the playlist and discuss how the lyrics relate to this week's study about Peter. My favorite is *You Are More*, by Tenth Avenue North.

CHRISTIAN REALITY CHALLENGES

Be alert to depression in others.

No music for a whole day.

 WEEK FIVE REPLAY

Peter probably thought his achievements would qualify him for a starring role in the new kingdom. Who else had walked on water? Who else had proclaimed Jesus as the Christ before the others? But God knew Peter was relying on himself, just as he always had. Jesus knew that Peter, even with all his ability and enthusiasm, would falter and fail. Only after doing the very thing he swore he would never do, did Peter have the humility to realize his profound need for Jesus as Savior. Only then could he become a real star—a rock solid enough to found a church upon—a rock star.

Sweet Jesus, Your love is amazing.
I can hardly believe that you would endure the unjustified torture
and pain of the cross for me. You even forgave your executioners.
I will never forget how much you love me.
Show me how to share your amazing love with others too. Amen.

WEEK SIX

ROCK STEADY

But you will receive power when the Holy Spirit comes upon you.

—Acts 1:8

PLAYLIST

Dive – Steven Curtis Chapman
Give Me Your Eyes – Brandon Heath
Get Back Up – TobyMac
Where the Spirit of the Lord Is – Chris Tomlin
Come Holy Spirit, Heavenly Dove – Isaac Watts
He Reigns – Newsboys

WEEK SIX PREVIEW

Thinking he was out of the running for Best Disciple, Peter returns to fishing. On the shore of Lake Galilee, God arranges a bittersweet reunion. This week we'll see how Peter's meeting with Jesus marks the explosive start of his stellar career as the church's foundation rock. Sometime between Easter morning and this morning, Peter had come to terms with his pride, his failure, and his need for a Savior. Nothing can stop him from diving in to get back to the Lord who loves him. With the Holy Spirit empowering him, Peter becomes the man of influence Jesus knew he would be. Pentecost showcases his inspirational voice and renewed commitment as he speaks to an international audience of thousands. Rock on, Peter!

Dear Jesus, Risen Christ, You are so personal. You ask us the tough questions. When you ask me if I love you more than others, what will I say? Have I learned to put aside my pride? I love you and simply want to serve you. Fill me with your Holy Spirit. Amen.

WEEK SIX, DAY ONE
DIVE IN!

Summer is swim time. If you've ever competed in a swim meet, you know the feeling of standing on the blocks, bent over, waiting for the gun or horn so you can maximize your leap as you start your race against the clock. Today we see Peter dive in for a race to the shore to speak to a very much alive Jesus.

Read Matthew 28:5–10. Who spoke to the women first? _____

Who repeated the message in verse 10? _____

The disciples had gone ahead to Galilee to wait for Jesus, who promised to meet them there. For most of them, the Capernaum area was home. God understood they needed time to process everything, time to reflect awhile on Jesus' teachings and the events of recent days. Getting out of Jerusalem also meant less immediate danger from the authorities they feared.

Seven disciples were together in Galilee, waiting, evidently clueless as to what to do next. Perhaps each one felt he had failed Jesus in some way. Peter quite likely was still embarrassed and feeling guilty for his triple denial, especially after he had displayed his inflated self-confidence to everyone at the Passover meal.

Now read John 21:1–14. How did this early morning fish-catch compare with that morning long before (Luke 5:1–11) when Peter had agreed to follow Jesus?

Similarities _____

Differences _____

Don't you just love Peter's reaction? As soon as John recognized Jesus—"It's the Lord!"—Peter grabbed his outer garment and dove in, racing the hundred yards to shore. This time, Peter did not ask Jesus to call him; he did not suggest that Jesus go away. No, this time Peter unselfconsciously got there as fast as he could. Compared to Peter's previous moments of great faith, how does this one show perhaps his greatest love for Jesus?

 CHEW ON THIS: *What makes you eager to spend time with Jesus?*

PETER: ROCK STAR FROM GALILEE

WEEK SIX, DAY TWO
BREAKFAST AND MORE

Read John 21: 8-11. All the fishermen finally arrived on shore to find Peter grinning and sopping wet.

What else did they see? _____ , _____ , and _____ .

What past events do those items remind you of?
Fish and bread _____

Charcoal fire _____

Nets full of large fish _____

There was Jesus, alive as ever, with a small fire (like the one in the high priest's courtyard), frying some fish and bread (like the boy's lunch that fed five thousand), and the disciples hauling in 153 fish (like back at the beginning of their journey with Jesus). It was such a great reunion. For a moment, it was just like old times. Jesus was back, the fish net was full, and breakfast was ready. They sat and ate with him, talking and laughing.

Now read John 21:15–17. What question did Jesus ask three times? _____

What answer did Peter give three times? _____

What response did Jesus give three times? _____

Why this three-fold repetition? _____

What did Jesus mean by telling Peter to feed and take care of his sheep?

_____

In this simple dialogue, we see no evidence of Peter's pride or ambition. Unlike his outburst at the Transfiguration or his cocky self-evaluation during the foot-washing, Peter makes no wild claims or promises. He has finally learned, even through his own failure on Friday, that striving to be the greatest disciple was foolish. It's not about him or his efforts or his intentions. It's not about his devotion, his eagerness, his courage or even his beliefs. Peter can only be his best when he follows, trusts, and submits himself completely to Jesus! Then, with the Holy Spirit dwelling in him, God can use him. Then he can be a star—a star that reflects the light of the Son of God.

Jesus is very gentle as he restores Peter to full discipleship. He seems to be saying, "Don't strive for greatness, Peter. Just love me and care for the people around you. Share my love with them."

CHEW ON THIS: *Why do we strive to be the best?*

CHRISTIAN REALITY CHALLENGE: *If you truly love Jesus, do something practical to "take care of the sheep." You did something like this in Week Two and Week Four. Can you do this regularly?*

WEEK SIX, DAY THREE
"I LOVE THE LORD..."

Because the Psalms often express strong human emotions, they can help us turn self-absorption into worship.

Read Psalm 116. It begins with, "I love the Lord, for he heard my voice; he heard my cry for mercy." In what ways might this Psalm have expressed Peter's feelings at this lakeshore breakfast with Jesus?

_____

_____

In John 21:18–19, Jesus warns Peter about how his life will go now that he is back on track. Instead of predicting Peter would fail again, Jesus seemed to know that now nothing would stop him. And Peter left his fears and pride behind for the rest of his life. He finally grasped that a steady love of Jesus and compassion for the world was all Jesus asked of Peter. This new steadiness would carry Peter to great heights. Let's see where God takes our rock star next.

 CHEW ON THIS: *How does pride often get in the way of loving and serving God?*

WEEK SIX, DAY FOUR
JESUS'S FINAL FAREWELL

Sometime after the beach brunch, Jesus gave all eleven disciples a parting word. Read Matthew 28:16–20. These words of Jesus are known as the Great Commission. A commission is a work order. For the disciples, it was their life mission. At this point, the reality of the resurrection had sunk in, and the disciples were ready to go on.

The commission has three parts.

A. Verse 18 confirms the authority on which Jesus speaks. How comprehensive is that authority?

_____

B. Verses 19–20a make up the commission. Where are the disciples to go? _____

What three things are they to do? _____

C. Verse 20b is his living, loving promise. Write it here: _____

_____

Do you think Peter was humbled by the scope of this assignment?
If this commission is for all believers today as well, how might it impact you?

_____

CHRISTIAN REALITY CHALLENGE: *Take the Great Commission seriously. What are some practical ways you can act on each part of this commission?*

A. _____

B. _____

C. _____

*This could mean taking an international mission trip. It could mean packing shoeboxes for Operation Christmas Child. It could include inviting a friend to Bible study. It could mean telling someone that Jesus really is God and he loves them. It could mean writing a song or poem about your faith. It might be a testimony in church about what God has done in your life. It could mean teaching younger kids in VBS or Sunday school.

HAPPY BIRTHDAY, CHURCH!

Jesus appeared to the disciples many times over the month following his resurrection. Each visit confirmed the reality: He is alive!

Read Acts 1:3–5. What did Jesus tell them would happen "in a few days"?

_____

And what did he tell them in Acts 1:8, just before he went to Heaven?

_____

How does this relate to the commission in Matthew 28:19–20?

_____

Pentecost was a Jewish festival held fifty days after the Sabbath of Passover week. Here's a math problem for you: If the Sabbath was Saturday, what day of the week would Pentecost always be?

_____

Today, Pentecost is celebrated seven weeks after Easter each year in most Christian churches. Let's find out why this date marks the birthday of the church.

First, read Acts 2:1–13. The disciples had been waiting for about seven weeks for this Holy Spirit. How did they know it had finally arrived? _____

What did they see, hear, and feel? _____

CHEW ON THIS: *How can we recognize the Holy Spirit today?*

WEEK SIX, DAY FIVE
PETER SPEAKS TO THE CROWD

Peter, transformed from drama queen to steady Eddie, now remained unfazed. He didn't get nervous or say something he might later regret. Rising to an occasion he could not have planned for, Peter simply stood to speak with the calm assurance of a man utterly convinced of the truth he was about to proclaim.

Read Acts 2:14–21, the start of Peter's speech before the international crowd. Which Old Testament prophet did he quote?

❑ Isaiah   ❑ Jeremiah   ❑ Ezekiel   ❑ Joel

What strikes you most about Joel's description of the latter days? _____

_____

I love how he says both men and women will have the Spirit poured out on them. Today, more and more we are seeing godly women speaking out eloquently for Jesus. There are many anointed Bible teachers who are proclaiming the gospel with the same intensity that Peter had.

Now read Acts 2:22–23. In verse 23, Peter highlights a very important aspect of God's work through Jesus. He says that Jesus was "handed over by God's set purpose and foreknowledge." Peter is saying that God knew all this was going to happen and that he used it for his pre-determined purpose. Wow.

Suddenly, all that Jesus had predicted came into clear focus for Peter, and he understood how God allowed every detail for a perfect fulfillment of his plan.

Verses 24 and 32 say the same thing in part. What is this truth? _____

In verse 33, Peter explains the amazing multilingual presentation. What was the cause?

_____

Finally, Peter brings his speech to a close with Acts 2:36—his post-resurrection confession of faith. It was the first time anyone had proclaimed the risen Christ, declaring him Lord. It was bold. It was powerful. How did Peter do it? He was filled to overflowing with the Holy Spirit. Praise God!

Those who heard this proclamation were "cut to the heart" by Peter's voice of authority. Upon Peter's invitation, they chose to repent and be baptized, so they too might receive the Holy Spirit. (Acts 2: 37-41)

In whose name were they to be baptized? _____

This was so important. From this point on, the early church added believers only through baptism in the name of Jesus Christ. It was, and is still, a sign of a willing commitment to follow Jesus.

How many were added to the church on this Pentecost day according to Acts 2:41?

_____

How does that number compare with attendance at your church? A church of over two thousand is known as a mega-church in America. How do you account for such immense growth in just one day?

_____

CHEW ON THIS: *Can the Holy Spirit give you the same kind of confidence and inspiration as he gave Peter? What would you do with it?*

The church was born. Jesus had told Peter, "Upon this rock I will build my church." And now he was doing it! His Spirit, speaking through Peter, was so attractive to three thousand that they wanted to be charter members in this new movement.

The rest of Acts 2 describes the values and practices of these first church members. List as many as you can find in Acts 2:42–47. _____

_____

What strikes you most about this list? _____

Compare this list of church activities with those of your church. What things are similar? What things are quite different?

CHEW ON THIS: *What would happen today if all churches were like the church described in Acts 2? What keeps them from becoming like this?*

WEEK SIX: INTO MY LIFE

How much do I love Jesus?

JAM SESSION

- What makes you eager to spend time with Jesus?

- Why do we strive to be the best?

- How can we recognize the Holy Spirit today?

- Can the Holy Spirit give you the same kind of confidence and inspiration he gave Peter? What would you do with it?

- What would happen today if all churches were like the church described in Acts 2?

- Which song from the playlist is your favorite? Why?

CHRISTIAN REALITY CHALLENGES

Do something to "take care of the sheep."

Take the Great Commission seriously.

WEEK SIX REPLAY

Peter's personal interview with Jesus on the beach was his personal turning point. Love Jesus—love people. That was all he asked. Peter understood the importance of the command and felt the significance of the three-fold repetition. From there, Peter soared on the wings of the Holy Spirit to great heights. His testimony, his enthusiasm, and his eye-witness authority brought multitudes to faith. God used Peter's personality and natural leadership skills to birth a mega-church in one day. How can God use you to further his kingdom?

Dear Lord, Fill me to overflowing with your Holy Spirit like you filled Peter. Use me in your plan to grow your church. What you did to give us a living Jesus is so awesome. Your resurrection power is more than enough for me. Let me go to my world and make more disciples. Amen.

WEEK SEVEN

ROCK STAR POWER

Salvation is found in no one else;
There is no other name under heaven given to men by which we must be saved.

—Acts 4:12

PLAYLIST

Angels Watching over Me – Amy Grant
In Christ Alone – Newsboys
Power of Your Name – Lincoln Brewster
All Hail the Power of Jesus's Name – Edward Perronet
Get Up in Jesus's Name – Lee Ann Womack
No Other Name – Unhindered
His Name Is Jesus – Big Daddy Weave
Our God – Chris Tomlin

WEEK SEVEN PREVIEW

This week we'll study some of the most exciting stories in the Bible as Peter discovers the power of Jesus' name and the wideness of God's love. Peter becomes the star he always wanted to be, but not on his own power. The supernatural power of the Holy Spirit works though Peter in miracles and eloquent speeches. He even opens the door to Gentiles through a divine appointment with Cornelius. Prison cannot hold Peter, and nothing can stop him from proclaiming the powerful name of Jesus Christ for salvation. There is a lot to cover, so hold on to your seat!

> *Dear Jesus, Your name is powerful. How shall I honor your name? I thank you for responding to all prayers in your name. Give me eyes to see who I may help through prayer in your name. Amen.*

WEEK SEVEN, DAY ONE
A CAREER TAKES OFF

Winning is only the beginning for the young person who wins the *American Idol* reality show competition each year. In many cases the winner, though unfamiliar with the music industry, finds record deals and performance schedules waiting. The new star has to be ready for whatever comes.

No, Peter did not win the competition for "Best Disciple," but when he was filled with the Holy Spirit, opportunities to demonstrate his discipleship came fast. God knows what we can do when his Spirit is in us, and "on that rock" he builds his church.

LAME, HOMELESS MAN PRAISES GOD, LEAPS FOR JOY

After the big church birthday party at Pentecost, Peter and the others had plenty to do in Jerusalem. They abandoned all thoughts of Galilee fishing for now. As the disciples performed miracles in Jesus' name, praise erupted from hundreds of new believers.

> Read Acts 3:1–10 for a particularly amazing encounter near the Beautiful Gate of the Temple. What did the man want? _____
>
> What did Peter and John give him? _____
>
> The lame man reacted dramatically to his gift. What did he do? _____

Much of the time we ask God for little things to make our life easier, happier, or more successful. But in this story we see that God wants to give us so much more! He wants us to look beyond the little things and be willing to change. He wants to change our lives from top to bottom.

CHEW ON THIS: *What could God give you that would make you get up and make a fool of yourself in front of everyone? Would you be willing to ask for that in prayer now?*

CHRISTIAN REALITY CHALLENGE: *Consider one of your prayers. If you are asking for something small, think bigger and be willing to stand up. When God answers your deepest prayer, praise him!*

Rock Star Power

WEEK SEVEN, DAY TWO
THE POWER OF THE NAME

The healed beggar was still leaping and screaming as a crowd surrounded Peter and John.

Read Acts 3:11–16. How was the man healed according to Peter? _____

Notice: The people running to Peter assumed he was a god. But Peter knew that his own power or godliness had nothing to do with it. The power was in the Name.

Many of today's Christian song lyrics talk about the power of the Name. There are several on this week's playlist.

CHEW ON THIS: *Why do you think it is important to remember where the power lies?*

Peter preached his second major sermon in Acts 3:12–26. Read it and take note of his remarks on the following:

Repentance (v. 19) _____

Restoration of everything (v.21) _____

Importance of listening to Jesus (v. 22) _____

Heirs of the covenant/blessing to all people (v. 25) _____

In this speech, Peter calmly explained that it is wrong to reject Jesus, the one the prophets spoke of long before. Peter pleaded with them to realize that Jesus was sent by God, and that he would one day return to restore all things. In the meantime, Peter stressed the message God voiced at the Transfiguration: "Listen to him."

WEEK SEVEN, DAY THREE
PETER AND JOHN QUESTIONED AND JAILED

Imagine a huge crowd milling around. Some have witnessed a great miracle. Others are afraid of a riot. A man is speaking boldly with authority about God. He is not a priest, just a regular guy, but he is very convincing.

Read Acts 4:1–2. Why were the priests disturbed by Peter's speech? _____

_____

FYI: Some people will always be disturbed when the crucified, resurrected Christ is proclaimed. If you think you can be a disciple and not cause some disturbance— think again.

CHEW ON THIS: *Why does the mention of Jesus Christ disturb so many people?*

OK, so Peter and John get to spend a night in jail. It didn't much matter to them. They were not afraid, and a couple thousand more believers were added to the church. No small potatoes. Morning came, and our heroes were brave. When brought before the Sanhedrin, the Jewish ruling council, Peter and John were asked just one question: "By what power or name did you heal that cripple?"

Read Acts 4:3–12, but read verses 10–12 twice. It's that good.

Did Peter change his story about how the man was healed? Where did the power come from?

_____

Verse 11 is interesting. This quote about the "stone the builders rejected" sounds familiar. Look back in Week Four, Day Three. (Luke 20: 17-18)

Who was the "stone the builders rejected"? _____

And who were the "builders"? _____

You see, Jesus understood how he would be rejected—arrested, tortured, and killed—but then become the cornerstone or capstone, the most important block in any building. Rejected and killed, he then was raised to a position at the right hand of God himself. And now, Peter knew what Jesus meant when he used the cornerstone verse. So he used it again. The Pharisees would remember hearing it first from Jesus.

Now read Acts 4:12–17. What astonished the men of the Sanhedrin?
- ❏ the courage of Peter and John
- ❏ the outstanding miracle
- ❏ their amazing authoritative speech
- ❏ how quickly this group was growing

ROCK STAR POWER

The "authorities" told Peter and John to stop speaking and teaching in the name of Jesus. Right. That was like telling the Beatles to stop singing. It was like telling the waves to stop rolling onto the beach. It was like expecting the weeds to stop popping up in my garden just because I said so. It ain't gonna happen.

Read Acts 4:18–22 to find out what Peter and John said. _____
_____

By now there were plenty of people talking about all these things. Welcoming Peter and John upon their release, the new believers immediately started praying. Read the last of their prayer in Acts 4:29–31.

When the believers were filled with the Holy Spirit, what did they have? _____

God is good. They asked for boldness to speak the Word and immediately they got it. Wow.

CHRISTIAN REALITY CHALLENGE: *Ask God for some holy boldness to speak about him. What do you think will happen? After you try it, share your results with another believer.*

WEEK SEVEN, DAY FOUR
MORE HEALINGS, MORE BELIEVERS, MORE TROUBLE

Model of Temple Mount looking East. Solomon's Portico runs
length of east wall between columns.

Solomon's Colonnade, or Portico, was the site of the first mega-church in Jerusalem. This is where Peter healed the lame man, and it became a gathering spot for all the new believers. Above is a picture of what the area looked like. It formed the eastern boundary of the Temple Mount.

Peter was becoming a hugely popular healer, much like Jesus had been. Read Acts 5:15–16 to see just how popular. At this point, Peter enjoyed first century rock star status. Being a rock star disciple isn't easy.

At this point, what do you think could be a temptation for Peter? _____

_____

 CHEW ON THIS: *What makes great spiritual leaders so vulnerable to temptation?*

Peter got to spend another night in the Temple jail. Questioned again, Peter responded similarly. Peter's first line explains why he and John couldn't stop speaking about Jesus.

Read Acts 5:27–40. What did they say in verse 29? _____

_____

Was Gamaliel being wise or just practical with his comments in verses 38 and 39?

_____

Peter had been flogged. Ouch. That hurt. They had spent time in jail and made enemies of some of the priests. And yet, when they came out this second time, what did they do according to Acts 5:41–42?

_____

Do you find that amazing? Fearless. They were absolutely fearless. In a few more years, each of these apostles would be martyred for Jesus. They simply never got over what God had done for them.

ROCK STAR POWER

ANOTHER PRISON CELL, ANOTHER ANGELIC ESCAPE

For a few years, the disciples managed to preach, teach and heal while avoiding trouble with the authorities. Then the persecution heated up again. Herod had James put to death and Peter put in prison again.

Read Acts 12:1–10 for perhaps the best get-out-of-jail story ever.

What did this angel do and say? _____

_____

What part of Peter's sleepy reaction makes you laugh? _____

In Rome there is a beautiful church called St. Peter in Chains Basilica. Ensconced in a glass case are chains believed to be those that held Peter. When I visited this church, I most loved seeing the wall mural depicting the angel leading Peter from the cell. The guards were sound asleep. I have always loved Amy Grant's song, "Angels Watching over Me," in part for the way she tells this story.

Perhaps the best part of the story comes after the angel leaves. Surprised, and wondering if he was dreaming, Peter went to one of the usual prayer-gathering places to see if anyone was there.

Read Acts 12:11–19. This scene could get a laugh on Saturday Night Live.

Who answered the door? _____ Then what did she do? _____

When they finally let Peter in, he matter-of-factly described his experience. The prayer circle was astonished, to say the least.

CHEW ON THIS: *Do you pray expectantly, or do you pray as a last-ditch effort, half expecting it could never happen? Would it make a difference in your prayers if you really expected an answer? Would you recognize the answer to your prayers if you actually got it?*

WEEK SEVEN, DAY FIVE
VISIONS AND VOICES, OPENING DOORS

Harbor at Caesarea

In the early days of the church, angels did more than help Peter escape. One directed a God-fearing Gentile named Cornelius to send for Peter. As an officer in the Roman forces, Cornelius lived in Caesarea, a beautiful city on the Mediterranean coast. (Locate it on the map in Week One.) Although not a Jew, Cornelius knew enough about God that he prayed regularly and was generous with his wealth.

Read Acts 10:1–8. If you had been Cornelius, would you have followed through with this? _____

_____

Meanwhile, Peter was visiting Simon the tanner in Joppa, another beach town about thirty miles south. God can work on the hearts of many people simultaneously. An amazing vision startled Peter just as Cornelius's servants made their way to Joppa.

Read Acts 10:9–16. Strange vision, right? Why did Peter recoil at the thought of eating from the selection he saw in the vision? _____

There may have been many "unclean" critters in the buffet, but read Leviticus 11:41–44 and find one clear command to not eat something that Peter saw. _____

_____

Peter was familiar with these food laws. Since most Gentiles did not follow these laws, most Jews never ate with Gentiles.

The voice Peter heard was teaching him something; even Peter the Rock Star still had something to learn.

What did the voice say in Acts 10:15? _____

_____

For Peter, three repetitions were usually necessary. (Acts 10:16) What were some things that happened three times to Peter? _____

Why do you think this vision appeared three times? _____

_____

Now things got interesting. In Acts 10:17–23, Peter sensed that the vision was about more than the day's lunch menu. So Peter got up and accompanied the three men and a handful of followers on the two-day walk to Cornelius's house in Caesarea.

Read Acts 10:23–26. What was Cornelius's immediate response when Rock Star Peter walked in?

_____

There was a day when Peter might have relished such treatment. But he had long since abandoned his ego, replacing it with a steady love and will to serve Jesus Christ.

What did he say to Cornelius in verse 26? _____

Why was visiting Cornelius such a big deal for Peter? _____

What difference did it make to the expansion of the early church? _____

_____

A large group of Cornelius's friends, after hearing about the angel's visit, came to see what would happen and to hear what this guy Peter had to say. So God had planned the meeting of these minds.

Now read Acts 10:27–48. Coincidences are not by chance.

Have you ever experienced something like this? If you have, did you think it was just luck or did you give God credit? _____

CHEW ON THIS: *Why should Christians always be looking for ways to include outsiders?*

Peter learned through this experience that God wants to include all people in his church. Peter learned that you did not have to be a Jewish disciple of Jesus to receive the Holy Spirit.

And so a *big* door was opened to the world. Whether you are from another religious tradition or no religion at all, God invites you to receive Jesus Christ. When you do, you belong to the family of Christian believers with the same standing before God. Remember that you were once an outsider, but now you belong to God. Thank him and invite someone else!

CHRISTIAN REALITY CHALLENGE: *Is there a group of people that is currently excluded from your church? How could that barrier be broken? Is there something you can do about it?*

WEEK SEVEN: INTO MY LIFE

Jesus is the only way to salvation, but the way is available to everyone.

JAM SESSION

- Which song on the playlist about the name of Jesus do you love the most?

- What could God give you that would make you get up and make a fool of yourself in front of everyone?

- Why do you think it is important to remember where the power lies?

- Why does the mention of Jesus Christ disturb so many people?

- What makes great spiritual leaders so vulnerable to temptation?

- Would it make a difference in your prayers if you really expected God to answer? Would you recognize the answer to your prayers if you actually got it?

- Why should Christians always be looking for ways to include outsiders?

CHRISTIAN REALITY CHALLENGES

Pray a BIG prayer.

Speak about Jesus boldly.

Be inclusive. Break barriers.

 WEEK SEVEN REPLAY

Peter, relying not on his own strength but on the power of the Holy Spirit, was able to heal a lame man by invoking the *Name* of Jesus Christ of Nazareth. And then he took some heat. Even when jailed, beaten, and threatened, Peter could not stop proclaiming the good news that Jesus Christ offers salvation to all. Completely in the flow of the Spirit, Peter was rescued from prison time and again by nothing less than angels. God was not about to let his servant die before his time. Prayer is powerful. When Peter set foot in the Gentile Cornelius's house after his wacky noontime vision, he paved the way for all non-Jews to become disciples through grace.

Dear God, Let me never forget how powerful your Name is.
Wake me up to the possibilities of your grace.
Help me change my world with the power of your Name.
Help me show your love and compassion to outsiders,
just as Peter did with Cornelius. Amen.

WEEK EIGHT

PETER. ROCK. LIVING STONE. STAR.

As you come to him, the living Stone—rejected by men but chosen by God and precious to him—you also, like living stones, are being built into a spiritual house…
—1 Peter 2:4–5

PLAYLIST

Living Stones – Michael Card
Living Stones – GodRocks
Live Out Loud – Steven Curtis Chapman
Cares Chorus – Kelly Willard
Come Thou Fount of Every Blessing – Jars of Clay
Chosen Generation – Chris Tomlin

CHRISTIAN REALITY CHALLENGE: *Burn a CD with your favorite songs from the playlists. (Be sure to get the music legally.) Use at least one from each chapter. Title it. Keep it. Share it. When you play it, let the music remind you of what you have learned about Peter, the Rock Star from Galilee. Share your selections with others. Tell them why you like those songs.*

WEEK EIGHT PREVIEW

About thirty years after Jesus' death, probably in the early to middle 60s, Peter wrote two letters to the widely scattered Christians throughout Asia Minor (present-day Turkey.) In the letters he encouraged them, gave guidance, and warned of suffering and dangerous teachings. He reminded them of the truth of Christ's teachings and the certainty of his ultimate return. Peter had given his life to ministry. The first twelve chapters of Acts tell of his powerful preaching and healing ministry, his managerial and pastoral skills, and his miraculous escapes from prison. But his legacy is contained in the letters he wrote. They confirm that Peter remained faithful to the end.

*Dear Jesus, Sometimes I feel so scattered. I don't feel connected to other Christians,
and I am actually afraid of being persecuted. What hope is there for me?
What does your Word have to say to me? What can I do when my cares are weighing me down?
Help me remember what you have already shown me. Amen.*

WEEK EIGHT, DAY ONE
LEAVING A LEGACY

If you could write a letter to kids entering middle school or junior high, what would you tell them? Would you warn them about bad teachers? Would you share some of your good experiences or your bad experiences? What do you wish someone had told you before you entered sixth or seventh grade? Would you tell them how hard it would be? Would you give them reason to be excited or scared? Would you share what you had learned?

Letters can be powerful. Of the twenty-seven books in the New Testament, twenty-one are letters. Most are letters to churches or large groups of Christians; some were written to individuals. In Revelation, Jesus himself dictated letters to seven churches and directed John to write and deliver them. Much church doctrine over the centuries has been formulated and debated based on these letters. The men who were closest to Jesus in those early years faithfully wrote letters of encouragement, correction, caution, and direction.

FLASHBACKS

While writing your letter to the incoming sixth graders, I bet you're thinking about the things that happened to you in sixth grade. When Peter wrote his letters, he was probably remembering some big events in his life too. Let's start by looking at some flashback verses in these letters. These are verses that remind us of events in Peter's life story—turning points or significant moments—in which he learned something important.

Try to match these verses to events listed on the right. All of them are things we have studied together.

1 Peter 1:13	___	a. Joy, even in prison
1 Peter 2:9	___	b. Jesus' crucifixion
1 Peter 2:24	___	c. "Peter, feed my sheep."
1 Peter 2:25, 1 Peter 5:2–4	___	d. "Peter do you love me?"
1 Peter 3:13–17	___	e. Falling asleep in Gethsemane
1 Peter 4:9	___	f. Visit with Zaccheus the tax collector
1 Peter 4:10–11, 1 Peter 5:5–6	___	g. Encounter with the Gentile, Cornelius
1 Peter 4:13	___	h. Transfiguration
1 Peter 5:10	___	i. Healing lame man by power of Name
2 Peter 1:16–18	___	j. Having feet washed by Jesus

Now think about which one of these experiences might have been most meaningful to Peter. Circle the one you would most want to tell people about if it had been you.

CHRISTIAN REALITY CHALLENGE: *Write a letter to a person like yourself, but imagine that you are much older and wiser. Seal it and save it for your own kids.*

PETER. ROCK. LIVING STONE. STAR.

WEEK EIGHT, DAY TWO
LIVING HOPE

Ever since that beach breakfast when the living, resurrected Jesus gently restored Peter's position and gave him a commission to "feed my sheep," Peter's hope and confidence remained steadfast. And the first thing he chose to write about was this living hope.

Read 1 Peter 1:3–5. How does Peter describe this living hope? _____

_____

_____

Our end is all good. Our future inheritance is kept secure for us in Heaven. Unlike an earthly inheritance such as an old, tattered quilt or a stock certificate that crumbles with age, our heavenly reward is preserved, imperishable, perfect, and shining, even more permanent that gold.

Read 1 Peter 1:6–9. By focusing on this living hope, what will believers survive?

_____

_____

And what will our response be to suffering?
- ❑ great rejoicing
- ❑ genuine faith
- ❑ praise and love of Christ
- ❑ complaining anyway

What does Peter say is the goal of our faith? _____

As the early church grew, the Christians faced persecution. Why? Established religions felt threatened by this new spirit-filled crowd that drew people away from idol worship and synagogues. Political rulers were suspicious of any "king" other than the Roman Caesars. So the combination of religious jealousy and political insecurity caused powerful leaders to round up and imprison Christians. But the first-century church was not weak. The Holy Spirit strengthened believers to the point of death. They were unafraid of suffering.

Peter's letter contains a verse that is comforting to all of us, even if we are not persecuted to the extent of the early church. Read 1 Peter 5:7. Write it here: _____

_____

_____

Kelly Willard wrote a simple musical tune using this verse called, "The Cares Chorus."

> *I cast all my cares upon you, Lord.*
> *I lay all of my burdens down at your feet.*
> *And any time I don't know what to do,*
> *I will cast all my cares upon you.*

CHEW ON THIS: *Why are Christians persecuted today? Does persecution have the desired effect?*

Even when Peter denied Jesus on the dark night of his arrest, when he felt hopelessly sinful and hopelessly unable to follow Jesus as he wanted to, Peter found hope to go on living. Where did that hope come from? Peter knew Jesus loved him. Therefore, he had hope of forgiveness.

Hope is a major theme in the Bible. Look up one or two of these great verses.

Psalm 25:5 _____

Psalm 33:20–22 _____

Jeremiah 29:11 _____

Lamentations 3:21–23 _____

Your reaction? _____

CHEW ON THIS: *What difference does hope make? When is hope the one and only thing you need?*

PETER. ROCK. LIVING STONE. STAR.

WEEK EIGHT, DAY THREE
LIVING STONES

You're familiar with the Rolling Stones and the Flintstones. You've heard of kidney stones and paving stones, but what are living stones?

    Peter uses this rocky illustration in 1 Peter 2:4–10. Who are these "living stones" and what are they being used for? _____

_____

    Why do you think Peter chose this analogy? _____

Draw a house in the space below, labeling the following parts as you understand them from this passage and from Matthew 16:18.

    Cornerstone
    Other building stones
    Foundation stone

    Besides being stones "built together" with other believers, what does Peter say we are in 1 Peter 2:9?

_____

PETER: ROCK STAR FROM GALILEE

Does this apply to you? Do you feel chosen by God? You are. Each living stone fits perfectly in place as the builder chooses the right stone for the building.

Following are some other verses that point to this same idea. Read them and jot down how it relates to the idea of living stones.

1 Corinthians 3:9 _____

2 Corinthians 5:1 _____

Ephesians 2:19–22 _____

Hebrews 11:8–10 _____

Psalm 127:1 _____

CHEW ON THIS: *How is God using you and your friends in his spiritual house?*

_____

In the hymn, "Come Thou Fount of Every Blessing," there is one verse that speaks of "raising an Ebenezer." Do you have any idea what that is?

Look up 1 Samuel 7:12. What did Samuel say when he set up this stone monument?

_____

Each living stone is also an Ebenezer, a reminder to others of how far God has helped us. Want to be an Ebenezer?

PETER. ROCK. LIVING STONE. STAR.

WEEK EIGHT, DAY FOUR
A LIVING FAITH

Peter had learned what it means to have living faith. He found sometimes you have to "get out of the boat" and sometimes you have to get out of the way. In other words, sometimes faith grows from stepping out of a comfortable, safe place into an insecure place where God will hold us up even in troubles. But faith also grows when we stop seeing ourselves in control. Peter couldn't be a star disciple through his own efforts. His ego had to go.

CHEW ON THIS: *What do you think you need to add to your faith in order to get get out of the boat like Peter did?* _____

And what might you need to add in order to get out of the way, to allow Jesus to work through you? _____

Read 2 Peter 1:3–11. What has Jesus given us according to verses 3–4?

_____

Think for a minute. What would it mean to you to "participate in the divine nature?"

_____

How do you think that might give you a living faith? _____

Below are seven character qualities that, according to Peter, make our faith effective and productive. Beside each one, rate yourself. (five stars = excellent, one star = needs work)

_____ Goodness: good deeds, upright
_____ Knowledge: time in Bible study, hiding verses in your heart
_____ Self-control: resisting temptation, holding your tongue, having self-discipline
_____ Perseverance: patience, standing firm in your faith even in trouble
_____ Godliness: reverence, love for God, obedience to God's commands, having godly traits like grace, mercy, forgiveness
_____ Brotherly kindness: warmhearted affection for people
_____ Brotherly love: selfless, sacrificial love for people

When I look at this list, I realize I have still a long way to go.

Lord, help me add these things to my faith, so I can be more effective and productive for you. Amen.

According to verses 10 and 11, what will you receive if you do these things?

_____

Peter knew that belief in Jesus as Lord and Savior is only the beginning of a Christian life. The more you grow in the character traits he listed in his letter, the more assured you'll be of your divine calling and your ultimate reward. Peter did not have all these qualities when he first decided to follow Jesus. But as time went by, he added them with the help of the Holy Spirit. You can too.

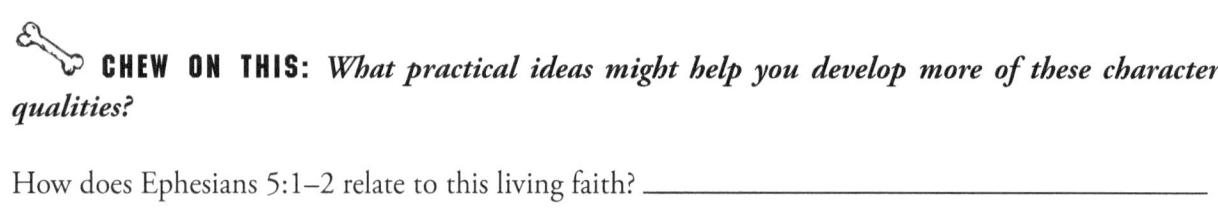 **CHEW ON THIS:** *What practical ideas might help you develop more of these character qualities?*

How does Ephesians 5:1–2 relate to this living faith? _____

When Peter wrote his letters, he knew his life was nearing its end. Read 2 Peter 1:13–15. Jesus had talked to Peter about how he would die. What did Jesus say in John 21:18–19?

_____

PETER'S DEATH

At the end of his life, Peter suffered shame and death for the sake of his Lord.

Peter was crucified in Rome. Many reliable sources attest to this including Clement, Bishop of Rome (AD88–97); Dionysius, Bishop of Corinth (AD180); Tertullian (AD200); Caius (third century); and Eusebius in his book, *Ecclesiastical History* (AD325).

He was martyred in the mid 60s under the rule of Emperor Nero, who was famous for violent persecution of Christians. Origen, an early theologian, wrote, "Peter was crucified at Rome, with his head downwards, as he himself had desired to suffer" (AD230).

But before he died, Peter made certain to pass on his experience and knowledge to the next generation of believers through his teaching and his letters.

PETER. ROCK. LIVING STONE. STAR.

WEEK EIGHT, DAY FIVE
FALSE TEACHERS

In his second letter, Peter warned about false teachers and prophets that plagued the believers of his day.

Read 2 Peter 2:1–3, 12–15, and 18–19. What are some things these false teachers do? List at least ten of them below:

1. _____
2. _____
3. _____
4. _____
5. _____
6. _____
7. _____
8. _____
9. _____
10. _____

The same things happen in the church today. Have you seen any of these characteristics in people? What do you do when you see such things? _____
_____

Peter wrote that in the last days, people would mock God's promises. Read 2 Peter 3:2–9. What quality of God does Peter emphasize in verses 8–9? _____

CHEW ON THIS: *Why does God not destroy all the wicked people and non-believers? How long do you think he will be patient?* _____

TRUE TEACHERS AND THE LIVING WORD

Throughout church history, true teachers have emphasized the Word of God.

One of my all-time favorite verses is Hebrews 4:12. Write it here, and memorize it if you can.

_____

_____

The Word of God was the force behind Creation. God said, "Let there be light," and there was light (Gen. 1:3).

Jesus was the Word of God made human. John 1:14 says, "The Word became flesh and dwelt among us."

And the Bible is the Word of God written by men, inspired by the Holy Spirit, and it is our way of learning how to live for God, how God is present with us, and how he has redeemed us through Jesus's death and resurrection. Paul wrote about the truth and value of Scripture in 2 Timothy 3:16.

Our friend Peter wrote this in 2 Peter 1:19–21.

What he means is that God controlled the writing of everything that is in the Bible, and we should pay attention. It is God's Word *to us*!

Read Ephesians 5:8–14 and again, 2 Peter 1:19.

"And we have the Word of the prophets made more certain, and you will do well to pay attention to it, as to a light shining in a dark place, until the day dawns and the morning star rises in your hearts."

Thank you for studying with me the life of this great man Peter, the foundation of the church. My final word to you is this: I too feel unworthy to be used by God to write this Bible study. Yet because of what Jesus has done for me and because I love him, I am compelled to share my faith and love of his Word with you. It is my sincere prayer you will hear God's Word to you, and that Jesus, "the Morning Star," will rise in your heart, making you strong, faithful, hopeful, and loving so that you can carry the living Word to your generation and the next.

WEEK EIGHT: INTO MY LIFE

How can I make a difference for Jesus?

JAM SESSION

- Why are Christians persecuted today? Does persecution have the desired effect of hindering the gospel of Jesus Christ?

- What difference does hope make? When is hope the one and only thing you need?

- How is God using you and your friends in his spiritual house?

- What do you think you need to add to your faith in order to get out of the boat like Peter did? What might you need to add in order to get out of the way, to allow Jesus to work through you?

- What are some practical ways you can begin to have more of the character qualities listed in 2 Peter 1?

- Why doesn't God just destroy all the wicked people and non-believers? How long do you think he will be patient?

- What new thing have you learned about being a Christian from Peter's letters?

CHRISTIAN REALITY CHALLENGES

Write a letter to a person like yourself.

Burn a CD with your favorite songs from all eight playlists.

WEEK EIGHT REPLAY

Peter gave up his fishing business to follow Jesus. At first he made plenty of mistakes. He wanted to be there to protect Jesus, and he hoped to win the Best Disciple award. When even his best intentions fell flat, he realized he couldn't do it by himself. Something finally clicked with Peter. I think it happened when he leaped into the sea to get to Jesus on the beach. He gave up his selfish ambitions and took on the commission Jesus gave him on the beach: Feed my sheep. From that point on, Peter was used by God, filled with the Holy Spirit. And God used him to heal, preach, teach, and open the door to the Gentiles.

Here are a few things I have learned as I prepared this study:
- Jesus loves me as I am, and he just wants me to follow him.
- Jesus really is the Son of God, who did amazing things everywhere he went.
- Jesus is always there to pick me up when I sink.
- My efforts to be the best will always fail when I rely only on myself.
- Even when I am most sure of my faith and loyalty, I might make a huge mistake. But it never will make me completely hopeless.
- If I love Jesus, I need to also love people.
- God's resurrection power is enough for me, and I can have it through the Holy Spirit.
- I don't need to fear persecution because Jesus is with me all the time.
- I am a living stone with a living hope in God's living Word.
- Like Peter, I can be a rock-solid disciple with God's help.

What have you learned from studying the life of Peter? I pray that you continue to learn and grow throughout your life by reading God's Word. Listen to what the Holy Spirit is teaching you. You can be a rock-star disciple of Jesus Christ, too.

Dear Lord, Thank you for loving Peter all the way. You knew what he could be when you called him from his fishing nets. You never gave up on him, and he grew into an incredible leader who made thousands of new disciples. Most importantly, you helped him see that only with your Holy Spirit could he do anything. I want to be the same kind of disciple. I want to love you and love people. Give me your grace and peace throughout my life. Help me become what you see in me. In the powerful name of Jesus Christ, I pray. Amen.

PHOTOGRAPHY CREDITS

Page

2   Fishing on Sea of Galilee: Library of Congress, LC-matpc-05162 and LC-matpc-07411/www.lifein-theholyland.com

3   Reconstructed 1st Century Boat: Todd Bolen, BiblePlaces.com

7   Views of Capernaum Ruins: Todd Bolen, BiblePlaces.com

10   Fisherman on Sea of Galilee: Library of Congress, LC-matpc-05166/www.lifeintheholyland.com

22   Capernaum from Sea of Galilee: Todd Bolen, BiblePlaces.com

26   Loaves and Fishes Mosaic from Tabgha: Todd Bolen, BiblePlaces.com

33   *Lord, Save Me!* by Norwegian artist, Mons Breidvik, 1921 (Altar piece in Norwegian Seamen's Church, New Orleans, LA)

50   The Upper Room, Jerusalem: Todd Bolen, BiblePlaces.com

60   Gethsemane at Night: Library of Congress, LC-matpc-03601/www.lifeintheholyland.com

66   St. Peter in Gallicantu Church: Todd Bolen, BiblePlaces.com

68   Antonia Fortress, Jerusalem: Todd Bolen, BiblePlaces.com

70   Garden Tomb outside Jerusalem: Todd Bolen, BiblePlaces.com

92   Model of Temple Mount looking East: Todd Bolen, BiblePlaces.com

94   Harbor at Caesarea: Todd Bolen, BiblePlaces.com and Library of Congress, LC-matpc-03998/www.lifeintheholyland.com

110   Sunrise on Sea of Galilee: Library of Congress, LC-matpc-05692 www.lifeintheholyland.com

Other studies by Sherree G. Funk:

Lydia of Philippi: Believer in the Lord

Joshua: Strong and Courageous

Ruth and Boaz: Woman of Excellence, Man of Honor

To order additional copies of any of Sherree's books,
or to offer feedback, visit
www.ServingOneLord.com

Serving One Lord † *Resources*

www.ingramcontent.com/pod-product-compliance
Lightning Source LLC
Chambersburg PA
CBHW051212290426
44109CB00021B/2431